THE *Pulpit*
AND THE
Punch Line

THE *Pulpit*
AND THE
Punch Line

**What The Preacher Can Learn
From The Comedian**

Jim East

ALDERWAY PUBLISHING

First published in Great Britain in 2017

Alderway Publishing
(an imprint of Emblem Books)
Ashill, Norfolk

British Library Cataloguing-in-Publication Data
A catalogue record for this book is available from the British
Library.

ISBN 978-1-908667-43-4

2 4 6 8 10 9 7 5 3 1

Printed and distributed by Lightning Source UK.

Contents

Introduction

Preaching and Comedy

This book explores the relationship between preaching and comedy.

Many sermons contain humour. The preacher's use of humour can range from a simple funny story at the start of the sermon to relax the congregation and/or give them a point of reference, to a wonderfully performed 'comedy routine' that engages and challenges the listeners in the midst of their uproarious laughter. Despite the commonality of preaching comedy, there is a dearth of literature,[1] both academic and popular,

---

[1] In the last 40 years or so, the publications have been few and far between. They have, in the main, emanated from North America and have included: Joseph M. Webb's *Comedy and Preaching*, (Chalice Press, 1998); most recently Bradley Rushing's *The Art of Using Humor in Preaching: Toward A Methodology Which Equips Pastors To Use Humor Intentionally In Preaching*, (Lambert Academic Publishing, 2010); Edward Rowell and Bonne Steffen's *Humor for Preaching and Teaching: From Leadership Journal and Christian Reader*, (Baker Books, 1998); John Drakeford's *Humor in Preaching (The Craft of Preaching)*, (Zondervan, 1986). Moving away from

on this broad subject area. More specifically, there is a lack of literature that investigates comedic styles and examines the potential of each for supporting a pulpit ministry.

In this book, I have attempted to select genres of comedy that have particular relevance to sermon preparation and the preaching event itself. Satire, black humour (in both the original and modern understanding of the term), observational comedy, improvisation, wit and physical comedy are all considered. The selection is, by necessity, contrived and incomplete – there are many more categorizations of comedy, and these can overlap and combine with each other and with the six I have chosen in an ever more complex way.

However, I hope that these six offer a succinct representation of a more far reaching study of comedy and preaching. Having made this choice, I have tried to set each genre in its biblical, historical, practical and, to some extent, moral context. The overall purpose of this exercise has been to create a text that encourages preachers to contemplate their own 'comic voice' and to hone

---

specific preaching texts: Frederick Buechner's *Telling the Truth: The Gospel as Tragedy, Comedy, and Fairy Tale*, (Harper Collins, 1977); and Dan Via includes a chapter on 'Comic Parables' in *The Parables*, (The Fortress Press, 1967).

its involvement in the proclamation of the Good News and the encouragement of God's people.

I have felt personally drawn towards this area of study for two reasons. Firstly, my experience of preaching has revealed numerous occasions when laughter has been a great blessing to both congregation and preacher alike. It seemed good to seek theological validation for comedy in the *preaching environment*.

Secondly, I have found myself to have only a few interests, but to be obsessive about them to the point of annoying those nearest and dearest to me! For example, cycling and swimming are now banned topics in our family home – my wife fails to see the importance of discussing derailleur gear ratios or the latest chlorine resistant fabrics.

Thankfully I have not been prohibited from discussing matters biblical and comedic, two more of my obsessions and more precious to me even than my bikes and the local pool. Biblical study and the resultant preaching are undoubtedly the most significant components of my ministerial week.

My time of relaxation is more often than not spent enjoying something from an embarrassingly large collection of comedies of many different styles, eras and mediums: films, sitcoms, sketch shows, radio recordings, books, comics and websites. I simply love good comedy and I love the effect that it has on my temperament, my relationships, even my preaching – I rejoice in an opportunity to take a closer look at the 'workings' of humour in the life of the preacher.

The book begins with a conversation that, while imagined, serves as a useful vehicle for answering the question, "What can the preacher learn from the comedian?"

Chapter One

An Imagined Conversation

In a casual conversation with a fellow minister, I mentioned an occasion when I felt called to use some comedy in my preaching at an evening church service. The chosen bible passage for the occasion was John 10:6-10 – one of Christ's beautiful illustrations wherein he refers to himself as, "the gate for the sheep." I had prepared a sermon focusing exclusively on the word 'gate', investigating many things that Jesus being 'The Gate' might mean.

However, as the service progressed towards the moment of sermon delivery, I became steadily more aware of a dour atmosphere hanging over the meeting. This unpleasant ambience was so noticeable by the time I was called upon to speak, that it felt as if an invisible barrier had formed between those in the main seating area and those upon the staging at the front of the church: musicians, readers, prayer and worship leaders.

Stepping up from my place within the congregation and passing from one grim side to the other made me long to see the barrier removed; if we felt disconnected from each other, surely a sense of worshipful connection with our Father might also be in jeopardy? I felt I needed to reach out to my brothers and sisters in manner that would be unifying in some way. How better than to invite everyone to laugh together with a good joke, or, failing that, a poor one?

It is questionable as to whether or not the joke bears repeating, but I shall do so, for the purpose of illustration only. In the most serious manner I could muster, I told everyone that my sleep had been disturbed the previous night by a young thief who was trying to steal our garden gate (as I said this I walked with the microphone back into the main body of the congregation); I steadily embellished the peripheral details of the story conversationally with those nearest to me until one of them asked me, "Didn't you shout out of the window at him?" This was my moment to reply, "No, because I didn't want him to take a fence!"

Perhaps a spiritual, emotional or some other barrier had genuinely formed and divided our gathering. If it had, then the moment of comedy (however strained or bromidic it may have been) seemed to permanently rupture it. Laughter came – much of it might have been in sympathy for my efforts, rather than as a spontaneous response to something hilarious – but with the laughter came a relaxed closeness and communication.

Perhaps I had entirely imagined the unpleasant atmosphere. If I had, then the joke was still very beneficial for me as the preacher – it helped me reach the point of proclaiming something I believed to be God's message *for the congregation* with a crucial personal sense of communicative connection *with the congregation*.

"I don't do comedy" said my fellow minister. The question is, should he? Does it have a Scriptural precedent?

In his letters to the emerging Christian Church, St Paul includes a truly inspired array of explanations, encouragements, admonitions and instructions. The subject of humour is not absent from his epistles and, arguably, neither is his use of humorous comments: it would be hard to forget Paul's opposition towards those who preached circumcision and his witty invective in wishing that "they would go the whole way and emasculate themselves" (Galatians 5:12); or how, after waxing lyrical to Philippian friends about confidences in his formidable Judaic heritage, he has no hesitation in dramatically changing his tone and vocabulary to describe the whole array of qualifications as *skubala* – literally, *dung*, but often

13

politely translated into the English as 'rubbish' (Philippians 3:4-8).

However, it seems that there were certain types of humour that met with scant approval from St Paul. In Ephesians 5:4, he specifically forbids "obscenity, foolish talk and coarse joking." There can be little debate over the translation and meaning of Paul's original words: *aischrotes* is filthiness, *morologia* is foolish talking and *eutrapalia* is inappropriate joking (possibly also used as a play on words to contrast strongly with his final comments on *eucharistia*, thanksgiving).

Paul's disfavour is entirely unsurprising and in keeping with his other writings. The Christian man or woman should steer well clear of the immorality that is so often either the fuel for comedy, or the sinister visage behind a comedic mask; but Paul makes no attempt to stop humour per se, or the laughter it engenders.

Paul wrote to a church that contained hundreds, if not thousands of Christians who had sat at the feet of Jesus himself and who had, doubtless, been entertained (or even humoured) by his use of hyperbole in dealing with the religious authorities: "You blind guides! You strain out a gnat but swallow a camel" (Matthew 23:24). Perhaps this faithful crowd had also been spurred to joyful laughter by Christ's satirical manner of story-telling (for arguments for and against Jesus' use of satire, see chapter two) and so a Pauline ban on all comedy might have jarred against their experience and their expectation.

Far from banning comedy, there is a specific occasion where it appears that Paul tries to marry it to (at least) the conversational proclamation of the Good News: 'Let your conversation be always full of grace, seasoned with salt (*halas*), so that you may know how to answer everyone' (Colossians 4:6).

Scholars and commentators have disagreed about the meaning of the Greek word *halas* in this context. The literal translation is simply 'salt' and many wax lyrical about its flavouring and preservative properties that symbolised goodness or 'denoted moral worth.'[2] Others cross reference this statement with Christ's call to be salt within the world in Matthew 5.[3]

Some, however, claim that it clearly means wit: Murray J. Harris explains that Paul is, "referring to

---

[2] G. Kittel, G. Friedrich, trans. G. W. Bromiley, *Theological Dictionary of the New Testament*, (Wm. B. Eerdman's Publishing 1985), 36

[3] R. P. Martin, *Colossians: The Church's Lord and the Christian's Liberty*, (The Paternoster Press, 1972), 139

pungency and wittiness of speech";[4] David
Garland gives a still more detailed explanation:

> In our idiom, salty language is something
> replete with profanities, but obviously that
> is not Paul's meaning. "Seasoned with salt"
> was used to refer to witty, amusing, clever,
> humorous speech. Their saltiness will
> prevent them from being ignored as
> irrelevant bores.[5]

Indeed, the New Jerusalem Bible of 1985
abandons any footnotes and provisos and directly
translates Colossians 4:6 in this fashion: "Always
talk pleasantly and with a flavour of wit but be
sensitive to the kind of answer each one requires."

It is, therefore, arguable that some aspects of
comedy – such as hyperbole, wit, and righteous
invective – might be employed in written or
spoken Christian ministry with Scriptural
justification.

---

[4] M. J. Harris, *Exegetical Guide to the Greek New Testament:
Colossians and Philemon*, (Wm. B. Eerdman's Publishing,
1991), 197

[5] D. E. Garland, *Colossians – The NIV Application
Commentary*, (Zondervan Publishing House, 1998), 274

"I don't do comedy" said my fellow minister. The question is, should he? Might it help him to communicate?

Achim Härtner dedicates a chapter of his book *Learning to Preach* to investigating the sermon as a communicative event.[6] Härtner carefully summarises some of the crucial observations regarding communication of the Gospel made by theologian Ernst Lange. He goes on to introduce Karl-Wilhelm Dahm's adaptation and advancement of the basic cybernetic communication model. Finally, he explains Friedemann Schulz von Thun's 'Hamburg' model of communication and emphasises its usefulness in analysing four key elements of both sending and receiving messages. According to this model:

I. *Each message has a 'content aspect'*. This is the specific subject information that is sent and received. When preaching, it is usual for this subject information to be of importance – maybe even of salvific importance – but, in the communication of humour the content might be singularly unimportant and disposable, for example, an untrue series of details about the theft

---

[6] A. Härtner, *Learning To Preach Today: a guide for communicators and listeners*, (Sheffield: Cliff College Publishing, 2004), 161-198

of a gate. One might question the usefulness of any message so lacking in content, until the 'self-disclosure aspect' of that message is taken into consideration.

II. *Each message has a 'self-disclosure aspect'*. The listener absorbs more than just information; our words communicate something about who we are and the receiver assesses us accordingly. Messages might reveal vast amounts of our character; even if efforts are made to make a message impersonal, it might simply disclose the sender's austerity, insecurity or reliance upon a professional persona.

The act of proffering, for example, a gentle, inoffensive joke gives a glimpse of the sender's desire to please or entertain and sometimes nothing more. This can be either a refreshing change for the listener or poorly received, but the vulnerable element of offering a humorous message that can be accepted with laughter or rejected with silence often garners sympathy. It might also prepare the way for greater communicative intimacy and it has the potential to remove any sense of arrogance, superiority or malice from the receiver's perception of the message sender.

In general terms, a message sender who wants to make the receiver laugh wants good things for the receiver: it's positive self-disclosure. In his book *The Psychology of Humor,* Rod Martin analyses numerous studies on the causes and effects of laughter; one of his conclusions is as follows:

> Taken together, these studies provide considerable support for the view that laughter is a form of social communication that is used to express positive emotions and also to elicit positive emotional responses in others. As such it seems to have an important social facilitation and bonding function, promoting and helping to synchronise and coordinate social interactions by coupling the emotions of group members.[7]

The self-disclosure of a spoken comedic message from the pulpit might usually, therefore, express a desire for bonding and good relationship.

III. *Each message has a 'relationship aspect'.* It seems, where humour is involved, that the self-disclosure

---

[7] R. A. **Martin**, *The Psychology of Humor: An Integrative Approach,* (Academic Press, 2006), 131

and relationship aspects of communication are intrinsically linked: a desire for relationship is part of what is being disclosed!

What we say divulges how we feel about the person, or people, we are saying it to and this goes beyond a simple hope of getting along – it might better be described as *a hope of purposefully getting along*. The preacher is commonly called upon to engage in biblical exegesis. In so doing, his "task is to cause the testimony presented in the text to be heard."[8]

This crucially important undertaking can lead the preacher to use comedy with this conscious or subconscious justification: "I am trying to be funny because I want our relationship to be sound; soundness of relationship will provide a good communicative atmosphere and this is necessary for you to engage with the sermon; engagement with the sermon is crucial because it is important for you to comprehend its message."

IV. *Each message has an 'appeal aspect'*. This begs the question, what response does the sender expect from the receiver of the message? Setting aside all aspects of the message except for the humour, it

---

[8] K. Barth, *Prayer and Preaching*, (London: SCM, 1964), 105

becomes an appeal for laughter, and laughter is no small expectation! Laughter is the momentary guarantor of attention; the fleeting proof of esteem; the softening of emotional barriers; the perfect precursor to sending the message of heavenly importance.

"I don't do comedy" said my fellow minister. The question is, should he? Is it, in some way, in harmony with the proclamation of the Gospel?

The extra-biblical history of comedy is both fascinating and fragmented. Aristotle makes note in his *Poetics* that, "The various stages of tragedy and the originators of each are well known, but comedy remains obscure because it was not at first treated seriously."[9]

This begs the obvious question, why were the stages and originators of comedy not initially treated with seriousness and painstakingly preserved? Aristotle subtly suggests that this could be because comedy found its source among the "phallic songs" of the poorer classes in the cities and because it is "a representation of inferior people."[10] Thus, he places the blame for vagary

---

[9] Aristotle, trans. W.H. Fyfe, *Poetics, Aristotle in 23 Volumes, Vol. 23*, (Heinemann, 1934), 1449a

[10] Aristotle, trans. W.H. Fyfe, *Poetics, Aristotle in 23 Volumes, Vol. 23*, (Heinemann, 1934), 1449a

upon the impoverished communities where he believes comedy found its roots.

Aristotle's lifetime (384-322BC) gave him a closer temporal proximity to the historical moments that he discusses than any modern student of comedy. It might, however, be the case that observing the modern nature of comedy can add further light to the issue of the gaps in its history.

Today it is possible to witness not only the fluidity of the multi-faceted world of comedy, but also its transience. That which is witty, daring and hilarious today is found to be staid, clichéd or stultifyingly unfunny tomorrow.

Comedy exists in an ever changing stream of fashions, culture and consciousness, and a distinguishing feature of comedy's existence might always have been its temporary nature. It is, by necessity, a chimera, built not of lion, goat and snake, but of constantly shifting elements, borrowed from wherever, whenever. The creature is incessantly being renewed and rebuilt as different ages, fads and fashions contribute a claw or paw to its shape. The creature is recognisable only by the laughter it generates. It dissolves and reforms many times in each generation.

Comedy captured by writing (or film, or ever more modern means) soon becomes no comedy at all. Often, all that can be gleaned from it is a glimpse of the age that created it, but the life blood of all comedy, laughter, is long gone – in all likelihood never to return. The study of comic history becomes by its nature the study of an exsanguine thing; perhaps Aristotle's antecedents realised this and abandoned the recording of comedy as a futile exercise.

And what of the laughter that comedy generates? Sometimes it rings out as an expression of joy in a pure and lovely form; sometimes it is an ugly or condemnatory sound that brings derision, hatred and disharmony. Dr Robert Provine is considered to be one of the world's leading researchers into the phenomenon of laughter; he has published the results of numerous studies investigating the processes which prompt laughter and the wider effects of it on individuals and groups; he comments:

> Laughter is a harlequin that shows two faces – one smiling and friendly, the other dark and ominous. Mardi Gras floats and sinister mechanical jokesters of old carnival funhouses mirror this duality – a volatile mix of gay and macabre that speaks to the emotional centres of our brain. Laughter can serve as a bond to bring people together or as a weapon to humiliate and ostracise its

victims. Despots have rightly feared its power and have savagely repressed it. Plato thought that undisciplined laughter could threaten the state.[11]

How can shape-shifting comedy – the sometime father of two-faced laughter – embrace and proclaim the 'ever-fixed mark'[12] of the Gospel? Was there ever so unchanging a thing as the Good News? Since its inception, it has been lambasted, attacked, outlawed and vilified, but it has not altered or faded away. Could there be more unlikely bedfellows than these two?

Nonetheless, comedy can be a messenger and the Good News is a message (one might even say, *the* message). It is the message that has frequently been delivered by those who have allowed their manner of annunciation to be shaped by the surrounding culture, just as comedy is shaped. Paul is unequivocal in his epistle to the Corinthian church:

---

[11] R. R. Provine, *Laughter: A Scientific Investigation*, (Penguin, 2001), 2

[12] Shakespeare originally coined this phrase in his exploration of love in the 116th Sonnet: 'O no! It is an ever-fixed mark, That looks on tempests and is never shaken…'

To the Jews I became like a Jew, to win the Jews. To those under the law I became like one under the law (though I myself am not under the law), so as to win those under the law. To those not having the law I became like one not having the law (though I am not free from God's law but am under Christ's law), so as to win those not having the law. To the weak I became weak, to win the weak. I have become all things to all men so that by all possible means I might save some. I do all this for the sake of the gospel, that I may share in its blessings.

1 Corinthians 9:20-23

William Willimon noted that, "Christian communicators readily used the Greek language that was available to them. Yet they did not accept the cosmology, the world which Greek language conventionally described. The language was seized and used for a very different message in order to construe for the hearers a very different world."[13] Could humour not be embraced in a similarly selective manner by the preacher?

---

[13] W. H. Willimon, *Peculiar Speech: Preaching to the Baptized*, (Wm. B. Eerdman's Publishing, 1992), 80

I believe that it is sometimes possible to detach the cultural eloquence of comedy and the comedian from its more unpleasant components (components that periodically offend or even run contrary to the Gospel of love and peace). Once it is free from indecency, comedy can be assigned a more heavenly task: to equip the "inculturating preacher" and to "enflesh the message of the homily, to clothe a declarative sentence announcing good news with the shared symbols and images of the gathered assembly."[14]

It is worth mentioning that attempts were made in ancient times to improve the propriety of comedy. Between the 4th and 3rd centuries BC, an Athenian dramatist and poet sought to steer comedy in a new and more morally acceptable direction. His name was Menander and he is commonly regarded as the founder and finest proponent of Athenian 'New Comedy'.

Emil Benecke said of Menander:

Indeed, the essentially "proper" character of the Menandrean drama is emphasised by more than one ancient witness. That

---

[14] S. V. De Leers, *Written Text Becomes Living Word: The Vision and Practice of Sunday Preaching*, (Liturgical Press, 2004), 100

Comedy could be anything but indecent was a revelation to Athens of the fourth century...[15]

How fitting it is that Paul chooses the works of Menander from which to select a culturally savvy quotation and include it in (once again) his first letter to the Corinthians: 'Do not be misled: "Bad company corrupts good character"' (1 Corinthians 15:33).[16] And how fitting for a word or two of Menander to thus be elevated to Scripture.

"I don't do comedy" said my fellow minister. The question is, should he? Do the various genres of comedy contain hidden lessons in preaching? What, exactly, can the preacher learn from the comedian?

---

[15] E. F. M. Benecke, *Antimachus of Colophon and the Position of Women in Greek Poetry*, (READ Books, 2008), 171

[16] This pithy quotation comes, in all likelihood, from Menander's comedy, *Thais*

Chapter Two

Satire

If satire is meant to reform persons, can there be such a thing as "cosmic satire", which probes the nature of humans rather than ridiculing the behaviour of individuals?[17]

G. A. Test

Researching the origins of satire and attempting to define precisely what is meant by the word are dizzyingly difficult tasks. Scholarly opinion is not simply divided, but rather forms a torrent of conflicting opinions that confuse and stifle any who wander into its flow.

  Sometimes the definitions applied underline the abusive and unpleasant nature of the form; at other times, emphasis is placed on the humour and the way in which it tempers the inherent

---

[17] G. A. Test, *Satire – Spirit and Art*, (University Press of Florida, 1991), 13

criticism;[18] some definitions expunge humour entirely, claiming it to be a non-essential element; others imply horror at the vagary of the way the term is applied to clearly distinct genres such as 'Insult Comedy' (see below);[19] still others do battle over the manner and means of satiric expression: is it purely literary, or to be found at the local comedy club?[20]

This looseness of definition has undoubtedly had an effect upon the theological understanding of Christ's use of satire in His parables and other teachings. Commentators Borchert and Stalker have no doubt that satire was entirely absent from all of Christ's words:

The love which governed all His feeling led of course to the whole gamut of irony, mockery, and satire being excluded from His speech... Kierkegaard gives it as his opinion that satire is justified as a weapon only in moral indignation, but that in such a case it is unnecessary. Yet the bite of satire

[18] See, for example, D. Griffin, *Satire- A Critical reintroduction*, (University Press of Kentucky, 1994), especially 161-184

[19] See, for example, D. Worcester, *The Art of Satire*, (W. W. Norton Publishing, 1969), 3 and following

[20] See, for example, G. A. Test, *Satire – Spirit and Art*, (University Press of Florida, 1991), especially chapter 1

is never without uncharitableness, too often bearing traces of personal irritation and bitterness; and so Jesus never made use of it when He spoke.[21]

Herbert Lockyer is just as adamant that satire is present in his monumental tome entitled, *All the Parables of the Bible*. In it he deconstructs and analyses some two hundred and fifty Biblical parables and calmly asserts Jesus' expert utilization of satire as a vocal tool. For example, Lockyer comments on Jesus' revelations regarding John the Baptist (Matthew 11:7-15) in this manner:

Thus with satire Jesus proved that John was not a man in whose life there was a prostitution of virility for personal pleasure.[22]

In the equally exhaustive *Dictionary of Biblical Imagery*, there, too, seems little debate about the presence of satire in much Biblical teaching, most notably Jesus'. The team of authors are happy to

---

[21] O. Borchert and L. M. Stalker, *The Original Jesus*, (James Clarke and Co., 2004), 265

[22] H. Lockyer, *All the Parables of the Bible*, (Zondervan Publishing House, 1988), 167

state that, "It is obvious that the Bible is a thoroughly satiric book"![23] Thankfully, they avoid most confusion by adding to this statement an impressive and simple definition of what they mean when they use the word satire: "the exposure of human vice or folly through rebuke or ridicule."[24] They go on to claim that all things satirical have four constituent parts:

I. *One or more subjects of the satirical attack.* Typically, the actions of the subject will have prompted the attack.

II. *A satiric vehicle.* The way in which the attack is constructed and delivered; for example, in the form of a parable.

III. *Satiric tone.* This, in turn, is divided between two spectral points: Horatian tone (light, subtle, humorous, poking fun at foolishness); and Juvenalian tone (angry, mordacious and caustic, attacking foolishness with more violence than the Horatian approach).

---

[23] L. Ryken, J. Wilhoit, J. C. Wilhoit, T. Longman, C. Duriez, D. Penney, D. G. Reid, *Dictionary of Biblical Imagery*, (Inter Varsity Press, 1998), 762
[24] L. Ryken, J. Wilhoit, J. C. Wilhoit, T. Longman, C. Duriez, D. Penney, D. G. Reid, *Dictionary of Biblical Imagery*, (Inter Varsity Press, 1998), 762

IV. *A norm.* Literally the standard by which all things are being judged, the point from which the attacked is perceived to have deviated and, therefore, the justification for the satiric engagement.

It is this definition that I feel it would be most useful to use to discuss some modern proponents of satirical comedy and the possible applications of satire in the pulpit.

In mainstream, contemporary satirical comedy, the subject of the attack is rarely in any doubt.[25] The target is usually a specifically disliked person or group of people; it can also be a person/people who are considered to be representative of an ideology (or organisation) that is perceived to be in some way flawed.

---

[25] On rare occasions, satire is so subtle in its lampooning of the subject that humour and irony are missed by the audience: for example, the 29th May 2002 edition of the satirical magazine *The Onion* contained a comedy article entitled 'Congress Threatens To Leave D.C. Unless New Capitol Is Built'; despite including the statement, "Look at British Parliament. Look at the Vatican. Respected institutions in their markets. But without modern facilities, they've been having big problems attracting top talent", on 3rd June 2002 the story reappeared alongside factual news stories in the international pages of the *Beijing Evening News*.

A good example of this is found in the 'Crime' episode of the satirical 'fake news' show *Brass Eye*[26] where writer and performer Christopher Morris sought to expose the foolishness of gangland violence, and those who take part in it. Pretending to be a legitimate and serious reporter, Morris targeted and set about interviewing former London gangster "Mad" Frankie Fraser (at the time of the interview, Fraser had spent forty-two years in twenty different prisons for a variety of violent offences).

The interviewee was oblivious to the increasingly humorous line of questioning which culminated in Morris producing an instrument that he described as "The Mad Frankie Fraser Madometer." This instrument was supposedly designed to measure anger on an increasing scale ranging from "Low Huff" to "Mad as a Lorry." Fraser was encouraged to give various hypothetical criminal situations a rating on the "Madometer."

The effect was, arguably, hilariously funny; but, for the preacher, even an attack on an *individual* advocating criminal behaviour is difficult to justify. There is a profound element of judgement inherent in selecting such a specific target for

---

[26] *Brass Eye*, created by Christopher Morris, 1997, DVD, 2 Entertain Video, 2002

34

satirical humour. Christ clearly warned His followers not to judge: "Do not judge, and you will not be judged. Do not condemn, and you will not be condemned. Forgive, and you will be forgiven" (Luke 6:37)

Moreover, he seemed disinclined to pass judgement himself, despite the fact the he had the divine wisdom and authority to do so: "You judge by human standards; I pass judgment on no one. But if I do judge, my decisions are right, because I am not alone. I stand with the Father, who sent me" (John 8:15-16).

Morris' task ended with his guest's behaviour *and his guest* publicly humiliated. A guilty 'judgement' had already been passed on Fraser by Morris and the television audience was encouraged to approve with their laughter. Like Morris, the preacher's task must, at times, involve deriding wrong behaviour (specifically, behaviour that is contradictory to biblical moral teaching); but, unlike Morris, the conclusion of the preacher's satiric message must extend beyond mere derision and include the offering of a Biblical alternative to the behaviour.

Sometimes the preacher's message might even include an attempt to illuminate the path of redemption for those whose behaviour is in question. To do this effectively it is nearly always more helpful to separate the wrongdoing from the wrongdoer (or, as St Augustine put it, we must speak "with love for mankind and hatred of sins").[27] For the preacher, selection of target is crucially important when using satire.

This begs the question: what is a scripturally legitimate focus for such humour? It would seem that pulpit satire can be reasonably directed towards confutative thought systems, standpoints and practices, rather than their adherents. The preacher also has the option of highlighting genuine or perceived problems in him or herself.

Self-effacing satire has the added advantage of humility in presentation (and the added danger of the preacher's reputation being undermined among congregational members who are not "in on the joke"). Paul undoubtedly targets himself satirically when he says, "By the meekness and gentleness of Christ, I appeal to you – I, Paul, who am 'timid' when face to face with you, but 'bold' when away!" (2 Corinthians 10:1).

For the pulpit, the choice of satiric vehicle is almost infinitely broad. Should a preacher so wish, he or she could construct a Madometer or some

---

[27] St. Augustine, *Letter 211*, (circa 424). Originally expressed as 'Dilectione hominum et odio vitiorum', broadly translated as 'With love for mankind and hatred of sins'

other humorous contraption. Or, more realistically, the onset of video projection means that a vast array of visual stimuli can often be employed: parable, story, reading an excerpt from an article as a precursor to comment, all present themselves as means of delivering satire.

It is little wonder that writer Ruben Quintero observes that satire, "has an unparalleled facility at cuckoo nesting in different media and genres old and new;" and that, "it should be no surprise that such an adaptive genre, somewhat existentialist in nature ... has found so many niches in popular culture."[28]

The same breadth of choice is available to the preacher regarding satiric tone. However, the selection of tonal proximity to Horatian or Juvenalian tone should be made with the greatest possible care. The subtlety of Horatian tone can make the message more palatable, but it can also increase the risk of satire being missed or ignored.

The more aggressive Juvenalian tone is swiftly understood, but might alienate or otherwise offend the congregation. Observing comedians, and the reaction of their audiences, analytically

---

[28] R. Quintero, *A Companion to Satire – Ancient and Modern*, (Blackwell Publishing, 2007), 9

can help in fine-tuning the preacher's own delivery tone. Broadus comments:

> The difference between skill and the lack of it in speaking is almost as great as in handling tools … mere practice will never bring the highest skill; it must be heedful, thoughtful practice, with close observation of others and sharp watching of ourselves, and controlled by good sense and good taste.[29]

Nowhere is this more apparent than in selection of satiric tone.

The preacher has an unrivalled advantage in establishing a norm in the minds of his or her congregation. The authority of the Scriptures on which the vast majority of sermons are based, their frequently unambiguous statements regarding Christian values, and the familiarity of most congregations with the principles and details of church teachings all go toward constructing a remarkably clarified Christian norm.

Such is the clarity of this norm, the 'faults' of worldly thinking are often spectacularly

---

[29] J. A. **Broadus**, *On the Preparation and Delivery of Sermons*, (HarperOne Publishing, 1979), 8

highlighted. In many ways, preachers should be the envy of comedians in having such distinct poles between which to suspend satire.

Chapter Three

Black Humour

The phrase "black humour" was originally coined by the French surrealist Andre Breton when he used it in the title of his 1939 collection of humorous writing: *Anthologie de l'humour Noir*. In Breton's own commentary that he includes with his anthology, he strongly implies that there is far more to black humour than poking fun at awful realities and creating an opaque screen of comedy through which one can dispassionately view the world. His first subject is Jonathan Swift, a man who (in Breton's opinion) defines black humour: "When it comes to black humour, everything designates him (Swift) as the true initiator. In fact, it is impossible to co-ordinate the fugitive tracks of this kind of humour before him ..."[30]

Breton goes on to compare Swift with his contemporary Voltaire in an attempt to clarify precisely what is meant by *l'humour noir*:

---

[30] A. Breton, *Anthology of Black Humour*, trans. M. Polizzotti (City Lights Books San Francisco, 2001), 3

In the same way he stood opposite Voltaire
in his entire way of reacting to the spectacle
of life, as their two death masks so
expressively attest: one bearing a perpetual
snicker, the mask of a man who grasped
things by reason and never by feeling, and
who enclosed himself in scepticism; the
other impassive, glacial, the mask of a man
who grasped life in a wholly different way,
and who was constantly outraged.[31]

Black humour, therefore (at least, in the mind of
the man who saw it as his task to establish it as a
specific genre) embraces a rage against society's
misplaced niceties and taboos. This rage goes
beyond any mere lampooning of selected societal
elements. Rather, it utilizes laughter to lay bare the
structures which allow bad things to occur.

It is fair to say that Swift employed myriad
different literary means to express his ire, and his
manner of expression ranged from subtlety to
vulgarity. His writing also periodically focused on
very personally felt wrongs and injustices. The
quintessential example of this occurred when
Queen Anne took offence at his *A Tale of a Tub* and

---

[31] A. Breton, *Anthology of Black Humour*, trans. M.
Polizzotti (City Lights Books San Francisco, 2001), 3

prevented his advancement in the Church of England. Swift responded in *Gulliver's Travels* by having his hero urinate on the empress's burning palace to save it from destruction. As one commentator noted, "Swift is especially fond of literalizing metaphors and turning them into narrative events."[32]

Similarities can be drawn between the darkly humorous *literary technique* of Swift and some of the spoken words of Christ. In the Lukan parable of *The Rich Man and Lazarus*, Jesus presents both societal inequality and terrifying divine judgement in the form of a parable. In so doing, He fixes these elements as narrative events and extends the narrative to include, for His listeners, a chilling and prophetic warning: "If they do not listen to Moses and the Prophets, they will not be convinced even if someone rises from the dead" (Luke 16:31).

While not being overtly funny, as a means of message delivery it is remarkably memorable, succinct, disconcerting and gracious. It is also expressive of outrage towards the fallen world – a world that has created 'sneering' Pharisees who

---

[32] C. Fox, *The Cambridge Companion to Jonathan Swift*, (Cambridge University Press, 2003),239

fail to grasp that, "What is highly valued among men is detestable in God's sight" (Luke 16:15b).

Highlighting the need to discover a sense of outrage and underlining the need to carefully express it could be black humour's most significant contribution to the preacher of the Good News. If all is well, why preach? If the world and the church are doing very nicely, then let silence emanate from the pulpit. But if there is much amiss, if the world is in desperate need, if the church is frequently tossed and battered on the tide of culture, conformity and sinfulness, then let the outrage flow, dark as it may seem and, maybe, let it be tempered by humour.

However, this seeming bridge between black humour and the preacher has been made tenuous by recent redefinitions of the term. Much has changed in the general perception of the genre over the last seven decades. At this present time, the case could be argued that the English descriptor 'black humour' is now being applied to an entirely different type of comedy. It could also be argued that this re-applied descriptor fails to accurately define the content of this type of comedy. A more useful and accurately descriptive term might be 'death humour'. Today's black humour nearly always finds its comic roots in human mortality. This harsh focus on our final physically moment is sometimes relaxed a little and laughter at death is replaced by laughter at suffering of one sort or another.

Should laughing at death and suffering be anathema to preachers of the Gospel? Such behaviour might initially seem inappropriately dispassionate for a servant of the God Who is "the Father of compassion" (2 Corinthians 1:3); and, after all, St Paul did call upon his fellow Christians to, "clothe yourselves with compassion, kindness, humility …" (Colossians 3:12).

However, Christ taught his disciples not to be particularly concerned about their personal physical suffering and death: "Do not be afraid of those who kill the body but cannot kill the soul. Rather, be afraid of the One who can destroy both soul and body in hell" (Matthew 10:28). And St Paul speaks of death utterly defeated by Christ when he quotes the words of the prophet Hosea: "Where, O death, is your victory? Where, O death, is your sting?" (1 Corinthians 15:55) and adds, "The sting of death is sin, and the power of sin is the law. But thanks be to God! He gives us the victory through our Lord Jesus Christ" (1 Corinthians 15:56-57).

Rather than leading to its dismissal by the preacher, perhaps such statements suggest that contemporary black humour might be of some use in expressing a biblical worldview of death; putting death in its place as something which is awful, but ultimately conquerable through Christ.

Far from making daring jokes, both modern and post-modern society has frequently seemed disinclined to engage with the subject of death and suffering. Sociologist Clare Gittings recently observed the following after surveying Western attitudes towards death:

> Indeed, it could be argued that individualism has now reached such a peak that nobody can face with equanimity the idea of their own annihilation, or that of someone close to them. Death has been hidden and forgotten as far as possible for much of the twentieth century; it is only recently that the taboo has begun to be broken down, for example, by the hospice movement.'[33]

Such a summary suggests a society that is very distant from much of Christ's pivotal teaching, most notably that which he offered just after Peter's confession of his messiahship: "If anyone

---

[33] C. Gittings, *Death, Burial and the Individual in Early Modern England*, (Routledge Publishers, 1988), 14

would come after me, he must deny himself and take up his cross and follow me. For whoever wants to save his life will lose it, but whoever loses his life for me and for the gospel will save it" (Mark 8:34b-35).

Enter contemporary black humour. The modern re-definition of the genre (or appropriation of the name!) underscores the fact that such comedy gathers its comedic momentum by probing areas that are normally left in darkness and not brought into the light of general scrutiny. In so doing, it frequently includes content that goes against the grain of what society deems to be acceptable, polite and fitting for discussion.

Thus, at a fundamental level, new black humour has much in common with the Christian Gospel. St Paul reminds us that a crucial part of the Gospel message is inherently offensive to many. In addition to this, Paul specifically seeks to preserve the "offence of the cross" (Galatians 5:11).

Does all of this imply that a preacher can simply add to his or her sermons offensive material that makes light of death or suffering? I would suggest not. It is a poor excuse and a tenuous link to state, "The Cross is offensive, therefore let my sermons be offensive too!" And yet I am certain that the daring and violative nature of new black comedy can inspire and help the preacher in his or her task.

I am equally certain that there is a time and a place for the preacher to ask shocking questions and make brutal statements, often not in the pulpit, but rather at the *work desk*.

Fred Craddock takes time to delineate a series of steps in the process of sermon preparation in his excellent book, *Preaching*. One of the steps is entitled, *First Reading of the Text* and within his explanation of the step Craddock asserts the following:

> This first reading is a spontaneous, even naïve, engagement with the text. *All faculties of mind and heart are open, with no concern for what one ought to think,* much less what one will say later in the sermon. This is the time to think, feel, imagine, and ask. All responses should be jotted down; do not trust the memory or take time to weigh the merits of your thought.[34] (Italics mine)

Craddock implies that there is a necessary time of private freedom that the preacher should have with the biblical text (or other sermon source). In this time, normal intellectual propriety should be

---

[34] F. B. Craddock, *Preaching* (Abingdon Press, 1985), 105-106

suspended and "no concern" should be given to what it is right and good and acceptable to think.

It is perfectly possible that such an exercise will generate blasphemies, unreasonable assumptions and much that is unwelcome in a sermon. It is equally possible that the preacher might be blessed with a profound moment of fresh thinking and insight into the text that will be valued by his or her listeners. It is this time of openness which might well be enhanced by the study of 'new black' comedians. It is they who observe the pain in the world around them and go on to make numerous open and outrageous comments about it in public; rather than jotting them down as a preparatory stage of speaking out.

As an expert in the delivery of new black humour, the comedian Chris Rock frequently offers a stunning array of jokes and routines about taboo subjects; in so doing, he gives utterance to many truths and highlights many injustices – he also causes enormous offence. Soon after the Columbine Massacre of 1999,[35] Rock incorporated a lengthy reflection on this atrocity in his stand-up show *Bigger and Blacker*. He begins the routine by

---

[35] Eric Harris and Dylan Klebold, both students at Columbine High School, Jefferson County, Missouri murdered 12 students and one of their teachers. They also wounded 23 others, prior to committing suicide.

explaining that he now refuses to share an elevator with teenage white boys and goes on to say:

> What the hell is wrong with these white kids shootin' up the school? They don't even wait 'til 3 o'clock either. Killin' people in the mornin', that ain't right! The Trench Coat Mafia. They're sayin', "No-one would play with us. We had no friends." The Trench Coat Mafia. Hey, I saw the yearbook picture, there was six of 'em. I didn't have six friends at high school – I don't got six friends now! (*expletive*), that's three-on-three with a half-court … Now everybody wanna know what the kids was listenin' to, and what kind of music was they listenin' to, and what kind of movie they was watchin'? Who gives a (*expletive*) what they was watchin'? Whatever happened to crazy? ... What? You can't be crazy no more?[36]

The routine is met by audible gasps as well as laughter from Rock's audience. Undoubtedly, much of the laughter is generated by the shock

---

[36] *Bigger and Blacker*, dir. Keith Truesdell, 1999, (DVD, HBO Home Video, 2000)

value that such a topic even be mentioned, but there is much in the message content that raises genuinely challenging questions. Are the claims of friendlessness and other excuses for such violent behaviour reasonable or blatantly ridiculous? Is the quest for a specific moment of societal failure (e.g. allowing the production and purchase of violent movies or depressing music) meaningless? Were the boys simply insane and not worthy of the elevated status afforded by everyone's interest in their 'psychological makeup'? It should all prompt a final question in the mind of the homiletician: can a similarly direct and aggressive and black comedic approach be taken when studying the scriptural text selected as the source for preaching?

Let us imagine for a moment that a preacher has been asked to preach on the widow's offering found in Mark 12:41-44. It is a poignant and inspiring account of an impoverished widow putting "all she had to live on" into the temple treasury. The woman's poverty meant that she gave (proportionately) more than all of the wealthy people who made their offerings alongside her, even though she gave less monetarily.

The passage seems, at first glance, to be presenting a challenge about sacrificial giving. Indeed, William Barclay comments that, "It may well be a sign of the decadence of the church and the failure of our Christianity that gifts have to be coaxed out of church people ... There can be few of us who can read this story without shame."[37]

But how would a comedian like Chris Rock read this account? Perhaps he might put himself in the place of the widow and tell his audience what he would have done with the two small coins other than put them in the Temple coffers: "Now hold on a minute, I got two coins, and this is all I have live on, and I can give them to the richest men in the country, or I can buy myself some food. I'm sorry, but Jesus is gonna have to show his disciples someone else, coz if they look at me, all they're gonna see is me walking past those coffers!" The old woman herself might come in for criticism for rank stupidity, "Maybe I should get a coffer and hang out nearby an old people's home in case any of them have been reading the bible?"

Odious as it might initially seem, what if this approach is absolutely correct and has, in fact, revealed a truth about this incident? If the woman was foolish, *or if she had been fooled*, then Jesus might have had a totally different intention in highlighting her actions to his disciples. Just a verse or two before the account of *The Widow's*

---

[37] W. Barclay, *Daily Study Bible, The Gospel of Mark*, (The St Andrew Press, 1960), 316

Offering begins, Jesus says these words to His disciples in criticism of the Temple's teachers of the Law:

> They like to walk around in flowing robes and be greeted in the marketplaces, and have the most important seats in the synagogues and the places of honour at banquets. *They devour widows' houses* and for a show make lengthy prayers. Such men will be punished most severely.
>
> **Mark 12:38b-40 (italics mine)**

If the subheading *The Widow's Offering* was removed and these verses were added to the account, it would cease to be a challenge to give more sacrificially and would instead become a scathing attack by Christ on the greedy authorities and their abuse of the poor. The men who victimize the underprivileged and the needy by "devouring widow's houses" are critiqued at the start of the account and then 'seen' in action at the end. As the perfect teacher, Jesus states his case and then gives his disciples a visual example of the truth of his words: they look on appalled as the shofar-shaped collecting chests[38] of the Temple rob even the poorest of what little they have, and this abomination takes place in God's Name.

Suddenly, with a little help from black humour, the passage becomes a wonderful starting point for a sermon on, for example, the prevention of cheating the poor and the importance of fairly traded goods, rather than a sermon that concludes with a supplication for more generous amounts on the offering plate.

It seems, then, that the original l'humour noir and the redefined modern black humour offer much to the preacher. The former might assist in finding a sense of rage against societal fallenness and distance from the biblical ideal, and in giving subtle utterance to that rage. The latter might assist in the uncovering of hidden meanings in biblical texts – black humour is a truly hermeneutical companion.

---

[38] The Temple had 13 'Shofar Chests' for collecting money. This was officially used for: shekel dues; turtle dove and pigeon offerings (where the birds were purchased with some of the proceeds and sacrificed); buying wood for burnt offerings; buying frankincense; buying gold for inlaying/repairing Temple décor; and six free-will offering chests to be appropriated as the authorities saw fit.

Chapter Four

Observational Comedy

Observational comedy is relatively simple to define, but rather more difficult to deconstruct! The humour is derived from the comedian accurately 'observing' various realities about the society in which we live. Sometimes the comedy centres on a specific age, gender or race of people; sometimes it centres on the family or working life; sometimes it centres on very specific collective social experiences, such as a governmental election; sometimes it centres on common experiences that are encountered periodically by most people, a visit to a garage, hospital, restaurant or church would all be good examples.

This style of humour is very common among stand-up comics and is so well recognized that some performers have parodied it and deliberately misused their observational abilities to excellent comedic effect. During his early years of stand-up comedy Steve Coogan created the character Duncan Thicket, also a stand-up comedian, but reliant upon cliché and possessed of a ridiculous voice and equally ridiculous wardrobe. In Coogan's 1994 *Live 'N' Lewd* tour, the Thicket character would actually announce that he was entering into a section of observational comedy:

> But the other thing that I do, right, is observational comedy, right. It's quite good that, it's where I observe something, right, and you go: "Yeah, that's true, that!" So, here's the observational comedy: right, right, right, have you ever noticed, have you ever noticed (it's observation, right?) Have you ever noticed, when you're walking along the street at night, you're just walking along the street, there's always someone, isn't there? on the other side of the road, that says in the top of their voice, "Hey you, y'four eyed (*expletive*), where'd you get that hat?" (*much laughter from the audience*) I think so, I think so. Oh yeah, one or two laughs of recognition there, that's nice! Oh yes, touched a nerve there![39]

Coogan succeeded in divorcing observational comedy from the way in which it usually resonates

---

[39] *Live 'N' Lewd*, dir. Dominic Brigstocke, 1994, (VHS, Vision Video ltd., 1994)

with personal experience; and, in so doing, he revealed numerous truths about observational comedy as a genre. If black humour probes areas that society intentionally keeps in darkness and obscurity, then observation comedy usually highlights truths that have been unintentionally ignored or taken for granted; or, more rarely, it launches an attack on common things that are unwisely done or cherished.

An example of the latter can be found in the work of contentious stand-up comic George Carlin. In one skit he highlights (among many other things) what he considers to be the average churchgoer's misplaced concern over dress code. In this famous routine, which is mainly based around espousing the merits of atheism, Carling includes some observational comedy while speaking of his reasons for worshipping the sun:

> Sun worship is fairly simple. There's no mystery, no miracles, no pageantry, no one asks for money, there are no songs to learn, and we don't have a special building where we all gather once a week to compare clothing. And the best thing about the sun, it never tells me I'm unworthy. Doesn't tell me I'm a bad person who needs to be saved.

Hasn't said an unkind word. Treats me fine.
So, I worship the sun.[40]

Overall, Carling's routine is little more than a vulgarized revamping of the most simplistic elements of the debate surrounding God's existence. However, by interspersing some accurate observations with foul-mouthed conjecture he gets many cheers and much approving laughter from his audience. That which might jar or sound unreasonable is hurried into the mind by sentences that resonate as true.

Used in this way, observational comedy might almost seem immoral. It's as if it's possible to introduce falsehood and conjecture into people's minds by sprinkling it with little truths. This is certainly not the task of the preacher of the Gospel. God's own Good News is inherently powerful and requires no subterfuge in its proclamation, as St Paul remarks, "My message and my preaching were not with wise and persuasive words, but with a demonstration of the Spirit's power, so that your faith might not rest on men's wisdom, but on God's power" (1 Corinthians 2:4-5).

---

[40] *You Are All Diseased*, dir. Rocco Urbisci, 1999 (DVD, MPI Home Video, 2003)

None-the-less, the preacher would be ill advised to ignore observational comedy as a suitable assistant in sermon construction. In a quite wonderful way, the human mind seems to react excitedly to a truth revealed or observed. There are several reasons why this might be the case.

Firstly, perhaps, it is the reassurance that unuttered feelings and concerns are shared and, therefore, validated in some way. The laughter is a vocal by-product of a sense of relief felt by the listeners.

Within a church setting it is very likely that the preacher, just like the congregation, will have plenty of these unuttered feelings and concerns. If he or she is able to periodically 'observe' some of them in a sermon context, then it gives an opportunity to apply scriptural support (or, if necessary, condemnation) to the observations. If the preacher's observations are in harmony with the experience of the listeners, a powerful impact can be made. Such an exercise demands a certain amount of vulnerability from the preacher and this, in turn, can also help to develop a more emotionally intimate relationship between preacher and congregation.

Prior to the construction of a recent sermon, I 'observed' that my personal prayer life was typified by speaking simple and accepting words.

I rarely, if ever engaged with God in a directly questioning manner. I interwove this observation into the sermon in a section about the disciple Thomas (also known as Didymus) and used his words and actions as an illustration to highlight the necessity of questioning God and being totally honest with Him – even if we feel awkward about doing so:

What do you think of 'Doubting' Thomas? Do you think we'll get to heaven and find him reviled and wandering about with a plaque around his neck that reads, 'DOUBTING Thomas'? I don't think we will. His honest questioning and doubts brought about wonderful things. When Jesus was talking to his disciples at the Last Supper he said many beautiful words, but it must have been hard to understand some of what he said: "Do not let your hearts be troubled. Trust in God; trust also in me. In my Father's house are many rooms; if it were not so, I would have told you. I am going there to prepare a place for you. And if I go and prepare a place for you, I will come back and take you to be with me that you also may be where I am. You know the way to the place where I am going."

I wonder how many of the disciples had any idea what Jesus was talking about?

But only Thomas dares to ask a tough question. He says, "We don't know where You're going, how can we know the way?" In substance he says, "What are You talking about? You've lost me!" Thomas' brave question prompts Jesus to say some of the most beautiful words in Scripture: "I am the way and the truth and the life. No one comes to the Father except through me."

You see, Thomas dared to ask the Saviour hard questions and wonderful things happened. Do we? I struggle with asking God hard questions sometimes. When I'm met with unanswered prayer, pain, suffering, vagary, I often mumble some prayers around the theme of "Thy will be done." I find myself praying safe prayers for fear of offending God. Am I alone in this?

Do you ask God hard questions? When something really puzzles you, you can't make sense of it, you just hate it, do you say to God, "What is going on? I don't get this."[41]

As it turned out, I was not alone. Several people spoke to me afterwards and admitted to being afraid to ask certain questions of God – questions that had been playing on their minds for some time. One person expressed mild horror that I should have failed to ask God difficult questions. He said, only slightly jokingly, "Shame on you, pastor, for not questioning God all the time" as he strode out of the door at the end of our meeting. As Duncan Thicket so wonderfully demonstrated, moments of observational vulnerability can garner mixed responses.

Secondly, it might be the case that the laughter caused by observational comedy is a joyful celebration of a new understanding of the world in which we live: it's precisely the same world, but there's a new perspective courtesy of the comedian's observations. Such a new perspective

---

[41] This excerpt is taken from a sermon preached at the Norwich Central Baptist Church evening service on 8th February 2009. The broader theme of the sermon was the way in which different Biblical characters and groups react in different ways to not understanding Jesus.

can imbue a listener with courage, an ability to endure, even a desire to forgive.

Comedian Bill Bailey produces a wonderful example of such laughter with one of the songs in his show *Part Troll*. In *Love Ballad*, he makes a series of pointed and pithy observations about the joy of romance and the way in which meeting a person and falling in love makes everything in the world seem wonderfully different:

And my life was turned upside down:

You showed me the beauty,

Of the things that I had never seen,

Like the snowflake that melts on the eyelash of a startled deer …

Or the duck that lands so clumsily on a frozen pond in winter.

But the intoxicating power of our love,

Transforms this simple act into an anthropomorphic drama,

Where Mr Duck's embarrassed and the other ducks are laughing,

"Quack, quack, quack, quack, quack"[42]

---

[42] *Bill Bailey Live At The Apollo - Part Troll*, produced by John K. Cooper, 1997 (DVD Universal Pictures UK, 2004)

As the audience laugh at these words and maybe feel a little embarrassed that they too have acted in a similarly sentimental way with a lover, Bailey suddenly changes the tone of the song and bellows, "And then you left!" Immediately the illusion of happiness is shattered and Bailey makes yet more observations, this time about the anguish of a broken relationship. Far from simply feeling a little embarrassment about sentimentality, Bailey expresses the complete change of worldview frequently experienced by the jilted lover:

And everything is turned to dust,

And everything is infected with a plague,

When you had to sleep with Craig…

The snowflake on the eye of the deer,

Has turned to pus

That oozes from an open wound;

The deer, now blinded, stumbles into a ravine.

The duck lies shredded in a pancake,

Soaking in the hoi sin of your lies.[43]

---

[43] *Bill Bailey Live At The Apollo - Part Troll*, produced by John K. Cooper, 1997 (DVD Universal Pictures UK, 2004)

The laughter from the audience is so plentiful that Bailey is forced to pause in his delivery of the lyrics by including increasingly lengthy instrumental breaks on his guitar. All who have suffered the genuine pain of betrayal or abandonment by a partner can laugh along with Bailey's spite-filled words and find, perhaps, some solace in them: "I am not alone in feeling this. If I can laugh about it, is it really so bad?"

Sometimes the preacher has an opportunity to offer similar solace from the pulpit. The underlying concept in all such sermon based observations is, however, more than a new perspective from the standpoint of humour. The preacher is not simply encouraging his or her listeners to laugh, he or she is reminding the listeners that followers of Christ are guaranteed a future glory that will make all present sufferings and dismay utterly meaningless.

St Paul stresses this in his letter to the Roman church: "I consider that our present sufferings are not worth comparing with the glory that will be revealed in us" (Romans 8:18). Instead of saying, "If I can laugh about it, is it really so bad?" the preacher should prompt the listener to say, "If I have heaven to look forward to, is it really so bad?"

This begs the question, is humour necessary to make such a statement? Certainly not, but it can help in reinforcing the correct perspective and biblical worldview. Bill Bailey could have simply encouraged his audience not to be worried any longer by lost loves. Instead, he led them laughingly to this important realisation, *and the laughter aided and abetted the realisation*.

In the same way, humour can add a 'sense of rightness' to a Scriptural truth that is inherently right. The generated laughter mocks the false worldview that had previously prevailed in the minds of the listeners. Just as the Lord's laughter mocks those who conspire against him and his holy plan for creation:

> The kings of the earth take their stand
> and the rulers gather together
> against the LORD
> and against his Anointed One.
>
> "Let us break their chains," they say,
> "and throw off their fetters."
>
> The One enthroned in heaven laughs;
> the LORD scoffs at them. (Psalm 2:2-4)

The preacher should be about encouraging the laughter that accompanies truth, rather than laughter in general. This is a fact that did not escape the attention of James Kendall, the author of a nineteenth century study on ministerial popularity:

> I would mention another sort of preachers, who are very popular because they make their hearers *laugh*. They say such "very funny things", as their admirers phrase it, that it is "impossible to help smiling". Now while we cannot deny that an occasional smile may consist very well with our edification under a sermon, particularly when occasioned by an *enlightening observation*; a frequent titter is both incongruous and profane.[44] (italics are the author's)

Thirdly, there is also the possibility that the comic observations serve as a reminder that some elements of God's creation are as they ought to be. In times of upheaval and change, great comfort can be drawn from observing and laughing at the routine, normal, unchanging parts of life. During periods of war or national distress, such humour

---

[44] J. Kendall, *Ministerial Popularity, A Lecture on the Popularity of Christian Ministers*, (Whittaker and Co. Publishers, 1847), 29

has been regularly found. One might call this selective observational comedy: that which is reassuring is highlighted by the observation and that which is worrying is belittled.

During World War Two, General Montgomery was placed in charge of the retreating British Eighth Army in Africa. He wasted no time in telling his troops that all retreating was done with, that he had burned all of the retreat plans, and that they were going to stand their ground. Montgomery then demonstrated his ability to selectively observe, in a gently humorous manner, in his first address to senior officers at El Alamein in 1942.

The situation was dire, but prior to doing battle with German Field Marshall Rommel, the infamous and successful "Desert Fox," Montgomery stated: "The great point to remember is that we are going to finish with the chap Rommel once and for all. It will be quite easy. There is no doubt about that. He is definitely a nuisance. Therefore we will hit him a crack and finish him off."[45]

Montgomery's message was simple: however dreadful things might seem, we always prevail;

---

[45] General Bernard Montgomery, discussed in S. Israel's, *Charge! History's Greatest Military Speeches*, (Naval Institute Press, 2007), 196

this is but a trifling affair and we shall soon have done with it. His speech is reminiscent of the words of the writer to the Hebrews:

> At that time his voice shook the earth, but now he has promised, "Once more I will shake not only the earth but also the heavens." The words "once more" indicate the removing of what can be shaken –that is, created things – so that what cannot be shaken may remain. Therefore, since we are receiving a kingdom that cannot be shaken, let us be thankful, and so worship God acceptably with reverence and awe.
> **Hebrews 12:26-28**

Whatever you might observe, some things are more worthy of observation! Even though the earth and the heavens are shaken, all this will do is reveal that which cannot be shaken, that which is of our God and Father. For Christians, statements of confidence in the Lord are more than mere bravado or hubris. However, the world can sometimes convince Christians otherwise. The preacher has an opportunity in the pulpit to make observations that clarify the hope-filled truth. He or she also has an opportunity to make observations that belittle the lies that stifle the truth.

So, observational comedy, by definition, points out what is already there; and sometimes it points out what is already understood, at some level, by the listeners. Fred Craddock extols the virtues of periodically constructing sermons that give a voice to the congregation; they benefit from hearing an eloquent summary of *their* message:

> This is in no way even a suggestion that one is to preach what people want to hear but rather a declaration that occasionally one should preach what people wanted to say. If a minister takes seriously the role of the listener in preaching, there will be sermons expressing for the whole church, and with God as the primary audience, the faith, the doubt, the fear, the anger, the love, the joy, the gratitude that is in all of us. The listeners say, "Yes, that is my message; that is what I have wanted to say."[46]

Just as there is little mystery over the reasons for the popularity of observational comedy. So, also there is little doubt about the potential benefits of

---

[46] F.B. Craddock, *Preaching* (Abingdon Press, 1985), 27

a sermon that recognizes people's deep feelings, offers a new perspective on the world, or reminds the congregation that God is on His throne and all will be well.

Chapter Five

Improvisation and Wit

The detailed history of improvisational comedy is practically impossible to trace. Of all genres this is the one where the comedic moment appears and evaporates most swiftly, made, as it is, from the observations and raw, unchecked, immediate reactions of the comedians.

Most scholars engaged in the study of the modern improvisational phenomenon follow its roots back to the Italian Commedia Dell'arte – a form of improvised comic theatre, traditionally performed by a company of ten actors. Dymphna Callery offers a snapshot of the 'Dell'arte' experience in her guide to physical theatre, *Through The Body*:

The Italian commedia players were masters of improvisation rooted in physical training, highly regarded for their skills and professionalism. Actors specialized in one stock character and improvised around scenarios, embellishing the basic plot outline with polished physical routines known as *lazzi*, (similar to circus or Music Hall routines), and virtuoso linguistic digressions (equivalent to the verbal riffs of modern stand-up comedians).[47]

It is, perhaps, a combination of the 'basic plot outline' and the 'virtuoso linguistic digressions' that are of most interest to the preacher; and it is these two constituents of Commedia Dell'arte that appear to be the most sampled and utilized in much modern improvisational comedy.

The writer Larry David followed up his successful show, *Seinfeld*, with a comedy series in which he is the star. *Curb Your Enthusiasm* is an improvised comedy show wherein David has tightly plotted the overall episode and individual scenes and then given his actors the freedom to improvise all dialogue within the plot framework. In this show, the freedom of speech extends far beyond actors simply having the choice to say a selection of normal things. David has included in his freedom of speech a liberty to abandon all inhibitions and to say offensive things that are far

---

[47] D. Callery, *Through The Body – a practical guide to physical theatre*, (Routledge: Theatre Arts, 2002), 61-62

from an accepted norm. The writer Lee Siegel noted the following:

> The expression of feeling, of sympathy, is often a reflexive response to the superego's socializing dictates, but the comic exists in asocial solitude: he's pure id. Which is to say, he's pure appetite. So it's no surprise that David's show is such a sensational success. In a society constantly cajoling everyone to gratify every appetite and impulse, David has burst the socially elemental inhibition that keeps people from surrendering to the impulse to say what they are thinking.[48]

Larry David has, in effect, said to himself and his co-performers that the plot framework is the only limiting factor on their words (that, and the producer's right to cut, re-shoot and edit scenes until they are considered funny enough to broadcast!). The simple gamble is that removing most constraints will produce something of greater comedic value, rather than a chaotic mess.

---

[48] L. Siegel, *Not Remotely Controlled*, (Basic Books, 2007), 69

As an approach, it has many similarities with Socratic midwifery: just as Socrates insisted that there was intellectual profundity within many people and that it was possible to allow it to be born;[49] so David has based his show on a belief that humour is inside all of his actors, just waiting to be given an opportunity for birth.

All Christians (not least, preachers) have been given a promise that something or Someone dwells within them. St Paul reminds the Corinthians, "Do you not know that your body is a temple of the Holy Spirit, who is in you, whom you have received from God? You are not your own" (1 Corinthians 6:19). It is essential for all who seek to speak on God's behalf to actively seek the guidance of the Holy Spirit. They must be open, not only to His leading during sermon preparation, but to Him actually giving a revelation of Himself during the sermon event.

With this in mind, preachers should seek structures and settings that are conducive to the Spirit's manifestation, in the same way that practitioners of Commedia Dell'arte and writers like Larry David create space for improvisation.

It is possible that the improvisational comedian's combination of plot outline and improvisation is

---

[49] See especially Plato's *Theaetetus*, 148e7-151d7

mirrored by the preacher's planned sermon and openness to Spirit-led divergence. However, the composition of improvisational comedy raises the idea that a preacher might plan a sermon with *deliberate* opportunities for fluidity and motion built in.

It could be argued that there is a danger this building in of opportunities for the Holy Spirit could become an arrogant and presumptuous process. It specifically presumes that God will manifest Himself in a particular way and within the 'plot constraints' of the preacher. Conversely, it is clear from Scripture that Christ himself has chosen his followers as a means of delivering the Good News and as implements of the Holy Spirit: "Therefore go and make disciples of all nations, baptizing them in the name of the Father and of the Son and of the Holy Spirit, and teaching them to obey everything I have commanded you. And surely I am with you always, to the very end of the age" (Matthew 28:19-20).

Therefore, it might be perfectly legitimate to seek opportunities for improvisation and to hone personal improvisational skills trusting that the Lord will make use of this in the same manner that He makes use of other styles of preaching. One might even hope, in so doing, that improvisation will be particularly in keeping with the action of the Holy Spirit: "The wind blows wherever it pleases. You hear its sound, but you cannot tell where it comes from or where it is going. So it is with everyone born of the Spirit" (John 3:8).

Many preachers have explored the benefits and Scriptural validity of improvisational preaching. Rather than basing their observations on comedy, jazz music seems to have been a favourite point of comparison. Robert Smith Jr. recently drew a lesson in preaching from Duke Ellington:

> Duke Ellington told his band members to play the notes as written but "to keep some dirt in there somewhere." By "dirt" he meant improvisation: spontaneous things they did not plan to do. The Holy Spirit deals in the "dirt area" ... The preachers' responsibility is to take people places they have never been before by being willing to go there themselves.[50]

Charles L. Campbell made a rather subtler observation when he discussed the way in which a preacher's personality is made manifest in the

---

[50] R. Smith Jr., J. E. Massey, *Doctrine That Dances: Bringing Doctrinal Preaching and Teaching to Life*, (B. and H. Publishing Group, 2008), 153

sermon, just as a musician's personality glimmers through his or her improvisational music:

> Preaching is not just an abstract language, but is embodied in the character of the preacher, the tone and inflections of speech, and the manner of delivery, just as a piece of jazz improvisation is inseparably related to the character and spirit of the musician.[51]

This creates a beautiful image with improvisation as its pivotal point. In the same manner that a jazz musician can absorb musical influences across his or her lifetime and then combine this with technical instrumental skill to produce a free and magnificent improvisation. So a preacher draws, from the world around, myriad influences, nuances and sources (divine and human, biblical and extra-biblical) and hones these with his or her 'technical' speaking skills and theological training to produce a sermon.

The question is, will this sermon be a rigid construction, or, like the improvisational musician/comedian, will it have a living, vibrant

---

[51] C. L. Campbell, *Preaching Jesus: New Directions for Homiletics in Hans Frei's Postliberal Theology*, (Wm. B. Eerdman's Publishing, 1997), 237

uncertainty about it? There are plentiful arguments in support of both rigid construction and improvisation and combinations of the two.

However, the improvisational comedy genre can do more for a preacher than simply encouraging him or her to sometimes improvise. It can help to make the preacher aware of a store of communicative information that grows within every person. Moving through life we find things that make us laugh and they are absorbed into our minds and, sometimes, find their way out in our speech. The unsuitable or vulgar things that we hear can be made more acceptable, the irrelevant can be made relevant, the old-fashioned can be modernized, and the foreign can be granted citizenship! Anything that brings us laughter can be cherished and shared – if we take the trouble to do so. And when we do, we potentially enter a truly blessed moment of conveyance where laughter as well as faith is shared.

All improvisational comedy derives from the comedian's lifelong process of collecting of humour. When called upon to improvise, they bring material out of their 'store'. Doubtless, some comedians gather their material unthinkingly, whereas others take great pains to record humour so that improvisation becomes easier and (in their opinion) more effective. One such careful recorder was television presenter Bob Monkhouse. He is a somewhat extreme example as he famously kept numerous detailed comedy files on a card system and effectively became an aggregator of all things comedic.[52] This allowed him, in 1998, to face the Oxford Union debating society and wittily deal with all questions, accusations and comments randomly put to him.[53]

While it is not necessary for the preacher to emulate Monkhouse's obsessive 'gag collecting' behaviour, there is great advantage in trying to embrace an eclectic mix of comedy. Jokes or witticisms can be retold from the pulpit in very different context. Obviously, the more obscure (or unlikely) the preacher's source, the less likely that the congregation will recognize it.

However, congregational recognition of source is no bad thing when including comedy in preaching (improvisationally or otherwise). I am a fan of the American cartoon *Family Guy*. When I very occasionally make use of the idioms of Peter Griffin (the main character in this cartoon) it

---

[52] See Bob Monkhouse's *Just Say A Few Words – The Complete Speaker's Handbook*, (Lennard Publishing, 1999), especially pages 76-80 for details of his painstaking process of recording 'gags'
[53] See *Bob Monkhouse On Campus*, dir. T. Kinane, (London Weekend Television, 1998)

generally passes unnoticed, but a few members of the congregation now look out for these brief quotations and make a point of telling me they have noticed. They are fans of the show too and they can usually pinpoint the precise episode from which I've borrowed a joke. I have found that this moment of recognition creates a more intimate relationship between preacher and listener.

The original scenario in which we first encounter a moment of comedy can be as important as the joke itself. Seeing where and how comedy fits into a situation helps to fine-tune improvised comedic responses.

A good example might be when a mobile telephone rings at a crucial point in a sermon. On one of the many occasions that this happened to me, my mind went to an amusing moment in the 1985 film, *Catholic Boys* where a pupil in a boy's school deliberately rings a telephone in a formal assembly, bringing it to a stunned halt. The pupil stands and theatrically answers the phone, announcing to the headmaster that God Himself is on the line, demanding that girls be allowed to attend the school.[54]

---

[54] *Catholic Boys*, dir. M. Dinner, 1985, (Optimum Home Entertainment, 2009)

When this moment of comedy popped into my mind, I wasted no time in saying to the culprit, "Answer that phone, it might be God telling me to shut-up!" The first time I used the joke in that context it got plentiful laughs and allowed me to continue preaching unflustered. It also allowed a positive 'breaking of the fourth wall'[55] that periodically erects itself between preacher and congregation. I've since used various versions of the same joke on several more occasions; I will soon have to search for another response!

The above examples are personal and very briefly representative of my unique engagement with comedy over the years. Each person steadily creates a comedic reservoir that is as singular as a fingerprint or a tiger's stripes. When the preacher dips into this reservoir and offers from it, it is like sprinkling 'touch points' into the congregation. Some people will respond to this revelation of self and the intimacy that it proffers. Others might ignore or be disdainful of it.

The comedic reservoir can manifest itself in other ways, most notably in a preacher's understanding and cultivation of wit. As a constituent part of many genres of comedy, the definition of wit is

---

[55] A phrase originally used to describe an imaginary barrier between actors and audience in a theatre with a proscenium arch.

nearly always coloured by its context. As an example of this, the 19th Century essayist Leigh Hunt investigated dramatic and poetic usage of wit and described it thus:

> Wit is the clash and reconcilement of incongruities; the meeting of extremes round a corner; the flashing of an artificial light from one object to another, disclosing some unexpected resemblance or connection.[56]

Hunt addresses much in his statement; but for many, wit as a modern, stand-alone genre has more to do with being succinctly, accurately amusing than with the element of surprise that was so enjoyed in previous centuries. The intellectual nature of dramatists and poets often led to a leaning away from the succinct and towards prosaic demonstrations of their humorous ability. It was the preserve of the 'common man' (or 'common woman') to say briefly what needed to be said and to engender laughter in the process. This directness is evident in the following Eighteenth Century account:

---

[56] L. Hunt, *Wit and Humor selected from the English Poets*, (Wiley and Putnam, 1846), 6

A divine, who had some years ago seen the poor in France eat a great deal of garlic, in consequence of his remark, advised the cultivation of it in a sermon delivered at Bristol... and advised the use of it to the poor at times when wheat was dear, and corn at a high price. For this counsel he was driven out of the city by the populace, and ever enjoyed the title of Dr. Garlick.[57]

In many ways, this working class humour of brevity has endured and the intellectual classes have appropriated it and called it "wit," with proponents like Mark Twain and Oscar Wilde, and more latterly Woody Allen and Steven Fry. A key facet of much modern witty comedy is that it must be as short and sharp as a pin and used similarly: to burst the unreasonably inflated egos, ideas and understandings that balloon their way about our society.

This acuteness can also be turned to less aggressive tasks of simply delivering much information swiftly and memorably. The Jewish singer and humorist Richard "Kinky" Friedman

---

[57] J. Almon, *The New Foundling Hospital for Wit – being a collection of fugitive pieces, in prose and verse, not in any other collection*, (J. Debrett publisher, 1786), 211

seems to capture today's concept of wit with a typically 'witty' statement:

> A person who takes a simple idea and makes it tediously complex, we call an intellectual. A person who takes a tediously complex idea and makes it simple, we call an artist. But if you can condense the whole megillah[58] into one line – then you really have something.[59]

The preacher who manages to include a witty statement or two in a sermon has at least three advantages in so doing. Firstly, it is low risk – a modern witty statement is concise and as such it has little impact on the overall length and rhythm of the sermon. There is no major investment of time. The sentence (or two, or three) can be delivered and abandoned as a tool if the congregation respond negatively or fail to respond at all.

---

[58] Megillah = Yiddish for an account that is protracted and tiresome in the extreme; worryingly derived from the Purim festival reading of the scroll of Esther

[59] 'Kinky' Friedman, *Cowboy Logic – the wit and wisdom of Kinky Friedman (and some of his friends)*, (Macmillan, 2007), 1

Secondly, memorability – in simple terms, it has been shown that there is an increased chance that people will be able to recall something they have found funny. Professor of psychology Peter Derks makes the following observation:

> From a direct perspective, humour has been shown to improve memory for shapes and for sentences over just meaningfulness alone (McAninch, Austin, and Derks, 1992-93; Schmidt, 1994) … It also seems to improve mood and flexibility of thinking …[60]

The preacher who would like his or her congregation to remember key facets of the sermon would do well to encapsulate some of those facets in wit.

Thirdly, ease of repetition – the same statement can be made again, perhaps without wit to further reinforce the point. Or, perhaps, it can be made again using a variation to the original humour. Woody Allen used wit very skilfully in his film *Manhattan* to repeatedly compliment the beauty of

---

[60] A.J. Chapman, H.C Foot, P. Derks, *Humor and Laughter: Theory, Research and Applications*, (Transaction Books, 1996), xviii

his co-stars Mariel Hemingway and Diane Keaton. Rather than simply telling them over and over of their beauty and potentially boring or alienating the viewers he chose to say things like, "I know my analyst warned me, but you were so beautiful that I got another analyst."[61] And, during his famous taxi journey, "You look so beautiful I can hardly keep my eyes on the meter."[62]

---

[61] *Manhattan*, dir. Woody Allen, Screenplay Woody Allen, Marshall Brickman, (United Artists, 1979)
[62] *Manhattan*, dir. Woody Allen, Screenplay Woody Allen, Marshall Brickman, (United Artists, 1979)

Chapter Six

Physical Comedy

Physical comedy can be divided into many sub-genres and the term is often used synonymously with slapstick comedy (slapstick itself originated from the afore mentioned Commedia Dell'arte and its use of a carefully manufactured, two-part slapping stick that could be used to strike a 'victim' with maximum force, noise and comic effect, and minimum injury).

In fact, physical comedy envelopes all things funny that find their comedic source in the physical. For the preacher, it would be unusual to include stereotypical physical comedy in a sermon. The pulpit is physically restraining, and the stage-striding freedom allowed by cordless or tie microphones seldom leads the speaker to perform a display of slapstick buffoonery. However, a closer look at the internal workings of physical comedy reveals much that can inform and benefit the preacher.

In his outstanding book *Comedy is a Man in Trouble*, Alan S. Dale quotes and amplifies the commentator and author M. Wilson Disher to clarify slapstick and summarise current expectations of physical comedy. They are a far cry from a sermonic norm:

> M. Wilson Disher claimed that there are only six kinds of jokes – falls, blows, surprise, knavery, mimicry, stupidity. They all play a part, but for comedy to register as slapstick, you need only the fall and its flip side, the blow ... Thus the essence of a slapstick gag is a physical assault on, or collapse of the hero's dignity; as a corollary, the loss of dignity by itself can result in our identifying with the victim.[63]

But, Dale goes on to make note of the fact that speech is, in itself, a physical act. With some obvious exceptions, physical comedy has always been ably supported by suitably adapted speech.[64] There is a marriage between the spoken comedic

---

[63] A. S. Dale, *Comedy is a Man in Trouble*, (University of Minnesota Press, 2001), 3

[64] The exceptions include medieval dumbshows, mime and the brief (early 1900s – 1927) period of silent movies where the music hall, vaudeville, festival, circus etc. performances were suddenly muted until technology could apply voices once again.

word and physical comedy; this natural coupling frequently gives birth to laughter and pathos. However, more than this, speech itself can take on physically comical attributes:

> There's also verbal slapstick to take into account. The term is an analogy, which generally refers to dialogue performed at a breakneck clip... the Marx Brothers' Broadway shows of the twenties and movies of the thirties, in which jokes come so thick you wish you had a court reporter making a transcript for you (as Groucho himself did, to preserve ad-libs for future use).[65]

Of course, verbal slapstick is not limited to simply increasing the speed at which dialogue is delivered. It can also include, for example: exaggerated speech content and exaggerated delivery; mimicry of those who are publicly (or congregationally) famous; putting on a strong regional accent; making use of an altered, stylised voice; or dramatic changes in volume.

---

[65] A. S. Dale, *Comedy is a Man in Trouble*, (University of Minnesota Press, 2001), 5-6

A preacher might, for example, make use of the simple tool of increased speed for increased emphasis – be it comedic or otherwise. By producing, not just words, but crucial pieces of information at a speed that is too fast for the majority to grasp, the final detail can be given unprecedented emphasis.

I witnessed the technique used with excellence once by a London market trader, in an attempt to sell radios he harangued his crowd by saying, "You might go down the road into *Dixon's* and pay eighty pound for this radio, (frantic pace begins) I'm not asking seventy pound, sixty pound would be a bargain, fifty pound would be givin' these things away, forty pound and I know you'd snatch me hand off, thirty or twenty five pounds, madam, keep hold of your money, listen to what I'm gonna tell you, this radio's so powerful it picks up the nine o'clock news at half-past eight, I've only got three left, (slowly) they are twenty pound today ladies and gentlemen."

A preacher might make use of similar method and say, "So what about poor St Peter? (frantic pace begins) he gets something right when he calls Jesus the Christ, he immediately gets it wrong when he tells Him to run away, he puts his foot in it when he offers to weave a few twigs together for Jesus, Moses and Elijah, when he tries to walk on water he sinks, when he tries to defend Jesus he only manages to injure someone's ear, he cracks under the pressure when questioned by a small girl, he's too busy crying to turn up at the crucifixion, he even comes second in the race to the empty tomb, (slowly) but for every time he stumbles and falls, he gets up and persists in following his Lord and Saviour!"

As another example of verbal slapstick, a preacher might choose to illustrate a piece of Scripture by adopting an exaggerated accent during his or her explanation. Biblical characters acting foolishly can undergo a process of characterization as they speak 'through' the preacher with an imbecilic tone. Likewise, characters puffed up with pride can be made to adopt lofty 'airs and graces' as their words or thoughts are spoken out.

On occasion, putting on an accent might aid the hermeneutical process in a manner other than simply underlining a personality trait. In Acts 2, we read of the amazement of the God-fearing Jews who witness the Pentecostal speaking in tongues. They go on (in verses 7b-8) to pass comment on what they have seen, "Are not all these men who are speaking Galileans? Then how is it that each of us hears them in his own native language?" It would be easy for someone reading/studying this

Scripture portion to miss the textual evidence that a *strong Galilean accent* prompted the God-fearing Jews to claim with such certainty that the disciples are Galileans.

The Holy Spirit had imbued them with an ability to speak perfectly the languages of the "Parthians, Medes and Elamites; residents of Mesopotamia, Judea and Cappadocia, Pontus and Asia" (verse 9), but he had not removed their provincial twang. How curious the original experience must have sounded, and how helpful it might be for a preacher to give his or her listeners a flavour of this experience by proclaiming, "Oui, sur mes serviteurs, comme sur mes servantes, en ces jours-là, je répandrai de mon Esprit: ils prophétiseront" in the broadest West-Country accent. [66]

Adopting an accent or being a mimic are undoubtedly skills that not everyone possesses. However, any lack of ability can be humorously made good by announcing the arrival of an impersonation to the congregation and including in this forewarning an honest confession of being a poor impersonator. A lame attempt is often more

---

[66] Any sentence, in any language, in any accent would suffice for this illustration! The example given is a French translation of St Peter's subsequent words in Acts 2:18, 'Even on my servants, both men and women, I will pour out my Spirit in those days, and they will prophesy.'

memorable and causes more hilarity and discussion than a polished, precise performance!

Modulation of voice can be complimented by an alteration of facial expression and other mannerisms. Many speakers and performers are masters of this subtle aspect of physical comedy. These mannerisms of the speaker do more than simply accompany his or her words: they constitute a means of communication in their own right.

Unlike the words that a preacher chooses, the attendant 'physical' expressions are a means of communication that transcend many communicative barriers. This has not gone unnoticed by those who are called upon to speak and perform; theatre practitioner Richard Schechner observed the following:

> But there are certain looks, sounds, and movements – certain facial displays, screams, laughs, sobs, crouches, stamps, and arm movements – which, if not universally understood, come close to conveying the same *feelings* everywhere.[67] (italics are the author's)

---

[67] R. Schechner, *Performance Theory*, (Routledge, 2003), 322

Comedians frequently exaggerate their physical expressions and present them to their audience for inspection: from Eric Morecambe showing his bewilderment by setting his glasses awry, to Tony Hancock's wild eyed 'double-take' – usually as he had a moment of revelation in the midst of a speedy, grumbling monologue.

This exaggeration makes it easier for a careful observer to associate such physical expressions with his or her own vocalizations. It also makes it easier to copy and assimilate them. In short, if a comedian has succeeded in sharing his or her feelings with you, they have also begun the process of teaching you how to share similar feelings (with a congregation or otherwise).

How valuable it is, then, for preachers to take note of the physicality of those humorous people who arrest their attention by making them laugh. At best, physical comedy can help to offer a preacher another channel of communication with his or her congregation. At worst, a lack of expression might render a sermon terminally dull:

Physical comedy uses body language to communicate humour. Facial expressions can be a great tool in communicating with an audience. A face with little expression has the same effect on an audience as a speaker talking in a monotone.[68]

---

[68] B. Fife, T. Blanco, S. Kissell, B. Johnson, R. Dewey, H. Diamond, J. Wiley, G. Lee, *Creative Clowning*, (Piccadilly Books Ltd., 1992), 57

Conclusion

The Power of the Punch Line

"I don't do comedy" said my fellow minister. The question is, should he? Can comedy have relevance when one considers the fundamental elements of preaching?

During my time as a school teacher, I became closely involved with organising and running seminars for trainee teachers from the local university. These students were asked to teach at my school as a part of their teaching practice placement and they were encouraged to reflect upon their experiences.

One of the seminars that I produced was entitled, "What does it mean to teach?" The seminar was based around an excerpt from W. G. Sebald's profoundly moving book, *The Rings of Saturn*. In this particular excerpt, Sebald writes in detail about a visit that he made to Ireland where he stayed in the decrepit house of the impoverished, aristocratic, Ashbury family. The family consisted of a mother and her three unmarried daughters. The mother is described in angelic terms as she repeatedly ascends and descends a set of mobile steps with tied bags of seeds to hang on the "much-knotted line that criss-crossed what was once the library."[69] The daughters are described as "giant children under an evil spell"[70] who sit on the floor of one of their many rooms, surrounded by vast piles of cloth which they seem to endlessly stitch into clothes and then unpick.

The excerpt concluded with the daughters, Catherine, Clarissa and Christina, showing Sebald the only piece of their needlework that had escaped the unpicking process: a bridal gown. Sebald describes the gown as, "a work of art so colourful and of such intricacy and perfection that is seemed almost to have come to life, and at the time I could no more believe my eyes than now I can trust my memory."[71]

I gave this excerpt to trainee teachers of all disciplines and asked them to read it through. I then requested that they write down what the passage 'said' to them – what they found most striking, what they found most challenging, upsetting or confusing. After a few minutes had

---

[69] W.G. Sebald, *The Rings of Saturn*, (Vintage Publishers UK, 2002), 211

[70] W.G. Sebald, *The Rings of Saturn*, (Vintage Publishers UK, 2002), 212

[71] W.G. Sebald, *The Rings of Saturn*, (Vintage Publishers UK, 2002), 212

passed, I encouraged everyone to take turns in sharing their reflections.

As might be expected, there was tremendous diversity in the interpretations of the passage. Biologists were engaged in a different way to mathematicians; students of literature were prompted to ponder in another way to physicists.

When the sharing of reflections had ended, the trainees tended to look at me to provide a definitive explanation of the passage that I had introduced them to, but that had never been my intention. Instead, I explained that Sebald was a teacher *par excellence* and that his skills were most ably demonstrated in the excerpt in front of them.

A good teacher takes his or her students to a place, a thing, or an experience and then gives them an opportunity to explore it; rather than bludgeoning them immediately with personal conclusions and thoughts. I continued by indicating that the room in which they sat contained a diverse collection of people, in just the same way that their classrooms would. In spite of this, Sebald had 'taught' in a way that reached them all.

I hope that this simple lesson was of some assistance to the students' continuing studies in understanding the teacher's task. However, it falls very far short of describing the task of the preacher. Rather than taking a congregation to a place, a thing, or an experience and leaving them to explore by themselves, the preacher leads a *flawed journey*, to a place of *greater reality*, and he or she is required to *engender a conversation* in that place. I believe that comedy has a contribution to make within each of these elements.

I. *A flawed journey*. Preachers are frequently described as being called to bridge the gap between biblical text and congregation/listeners.[72] To do this they must, themselves, make a journey into the biblical text and attempt to *personally* discover its meaning – this is one of the first stages of the journey to bring the message to the congregation. In some ways, this journey that the preacher makes into the text takes place within the confines of surprisingly narrow parameters.

To understand what a text is saying to *you*, you must possess some understanding of who *you* are! A lack of self-comprehension leads to problems

---

[72] See, for example: T.G. Long, *The Witness of Preaching*, (Westminster John Knox Press, 2005), introduction, chapters 1, 4, 10; J.R.W. Stott, *I Believe in Preaching* (Hodder and Stoughton, 1982), chapter 4; F.B. Craddock, *Preaching* (Abingdon Press, 1985), chapters 1, 3, 5, 7, 11; P. Ricoeur, *The Conflict of Interpretations: Essays in Hermeneutics*, (Northwestern University Press, 2007), Existence and Hermeneutics

comprehending the message of a Biblical text in a personal way. A little worryingly, St Paul implies that we are universally flawed and incomplete in our self-comprehension: "Now we see but a poor reflection as in a mirror; then we shall see face to face. Now I know in part; then I shall know fully, *even as I am fully known*" (1 Corinthians 13:12, italics mine).

The preacher, therefore, takes his or her partial/flawed self-comprehension, interprets the text accordingly and invites the congregation to join him or her on a potentially flawed journey into the text. Paul Ricoeur emphasises the journey and its reliance upon self-comprehension in his essay collection, *The Conflict of Interpretations*:

And finally, the very work of interpretation reveals a profound intention, that of overcoming distance and cultural differences and of matching the reader to a text which has become foreign, thereby incorporating its meaning into the *present comprehension* a man is able to have of himself.[73] (italics mine)

---

[73] P. Ricoeur, *The Conflict of Interpretations: Essays in Hermeneutics*, (Northwestern University Press, 2007), 4

Flawed and connected to our current human imperfection of self-knowledge as the interpretive aspect of the preaching journey might be, there is much to encourage us. It is a journey that Christ himself has called us to make, because he himself calls us to preach: "Go into all the world and preach the good news to all creation" (Mark 16:15).

This suggests that any shortfall in our abilities is not an insurmountable problem and might even be a means of the Lord manifesting his grace by being strong in our weakness. One of his messages to St Paul clearly demonstrates his sovereign choice to sometimes act in this way: "But he said to me, 'My grace is sufficient for you, for my power is made perfect in weakness'" (2 Corinthians 12:9a).

We can be further reassured by the fact that we are not called to actually preach knowledgeably about ourselves: "For we do not preach ourselves, but Jesus Christ as Lord, and ourselves as your servants for Jesus' sake" (2 Corinthians 4:5). Self-knowledge is part of the mechanism of delivery, but not the core of the message itself.

Nevertheless, there must be a response by the preacher to the received wisdom that we are not wise about ourselves. How should we react to the deficit in our present comprehension? St James suggests that heavenly wisdom leads to humility: "Who is wise and understanding among you? Let him show it by his good life, by deeds done in the humility that comes from wisdom." In humility, then, the preacher can accept his or her lack of self-knowledge. It is in engendering humility that comedy has a crucial role to play.

Arrogance and pride are often accompanied by a lack of humour, or, more specifically, a lack of ability to laugh at oneself. Theologian Jean-Jacques Suurmond observed that, "Dictators are notorious for their lack of a sense of humour and inability to relativize themselves …"[74]

By the opposite measure, the ability to examine one's life without a sense of pomposity or hubris is ably supported by self-deprecating humour. To laugh at oneself, a person must entertain the possibility that he or she is faintly (or distinctly) ridiculous in some way. A person must accept that this ridiculousness is difficult to disguise and might prompt mocking laughter at any point of interaction with others. A person must be humble enough to join with the mockers and assume so little of him or herself that they can amplify the general laughter with their own.

Some consider such an ability to be indicative of moral health and an aid towards achieving it. In

---

[74] J. Suurmond, *Word and Spirit at Play: Towards a Charismatic Theology*, (Wm. B. Eerdman's Publishing, 1995), 127

The Morality of Laughter, F.H. Buckley calls attention to this notion:

> Hypocrisy is the Queen of the comic vices, and few things are as pleasureful [*sic*] as the delight we take in mocking the hypocrite. We desperately need such laughter, for no vice is quite so beguiling. We always see the mote in another's eye, ignoring the beam in our own. How could it be otherwise, *cher hypocrite, mon semblance*, when our self-love is so strong? Who could bear to know what others think of one, or (what is worse) how seldom they think of one? Our capacity to delude ourselves is infinite, and it is never so strong as when we think we have at last achieved self-knowledge.[75] (italics are the author's)

It is, therefore, beneficial for a preacher to learn to laugh, and most importantly to learn to laugh at him or herself. Such an ability allows the preacher to sidestep some of the issues caused by a lack of self-knowledge. For example, when beginning the journey into interpreting a biblical text, the

---

[75] F.H. Buckley, *The Morality of Laughter*, (University of Michigan Press, 2005), 95

preacher might encounter a word of chastisement or challenge in the Scriptures. If he or she is able to laugh at him or herself, there is an increased likelihood that the word will be humbly taken on board as a personal message to share, rather than an impersonal message to announce.

Thus, the preacher moves further from a Pharisaical approach and closer to the approach of the justified tax collector (Luke 18:9-14). Furthermore, in assuming a degree of personal ludicrousness, one is doing the equivalent of choosing the lowest place at the banqueting table and raising the possibility of being elevated by the Host (Luke 14:7-11). This elevation might even include the heady privilege of speaking on behalf of the Host at a gathering of His people.

II. *A place of greater reality.* How tempting it is for a preacher to adopt the role of a heavenly travel agent, providing short breaks away from the loathsome drudgery of everyday life. "Worries about your jobs, concerns about daily chores, painful or difficult relationships, all of these and more can be left outside the door of this church! Welcome to a divine preaching experience that will make you forget all of your cares and transport you, albeit briefly, to a place where reality is put on hold for an hour or so …"

People can listen to a sermon and feel good, feel encouraged and feel rested from the 'real'.

Or should it sometimes be the case that a sermon ought to amplify the reality of daily life? But what if daily life contained only shards or vague reflections of reality? Maybe a sermon should, therefore, reveal a greater reality from the biblical narrative and demand that the listeners adjust all things to comply with its truths? In *Mimesis*, Erich Auerbach notes:

> Far from seeking, like Homer, merely to make us forget our own reality for a few hours, [the biblical narrative] seeks to overcome our reality: we are to fit our own life into its world, feel ourselves to be elements in its structure of universal history.[76]

This is a far cry from escapism – defined broadly as "the tendency to seek distraction and relief from reality"[77] – the sermon must imply that ultimate reality and relief are synonymous and that

---

[76] E. Auerbach, Trans. W.R. Trask, *Mimesis: The Representation of Reality in Western Literature*, (Princeton University Press, 1968), p15
[77] Oxford English Dictionary

distraction from ultimate reality is deeply spiritually harmful.

The sermon could be seen as being paradoxical in the initial stages of its delivery. It has elements commonly associated with the ethereal in that it is profoundly supernal, holy and 'other' because of its claim and calling to deliver the message of the divine. And yet, and at the same time, it deals with sobering and absolute truth and is earthbound as a result of being spoken by a man or woman.

However, the time of paradoxical existence is potentially short-lived. When the Lord graciously chooses to make use of a sermon, it is almost as if the heavenly message arrives encased in a lesser reality that crumbles and falls away as the sermon event comes to fruition. This process found embodiment in the relationship between Christ and John the Baptist. The Baptist realized that the waning of his ministry was an essential part of Christ's growing ministry: "The bride belongs to the bridegroom. The friend who attends the bridegroom waits and listens for him, and is full of joy when he hears the bridegroom's voice. That joy is mine, and it is now complete. He must become greater; I must become less" (John 3:29-30).

Everything that John had announced had been 'real' enough. But there came a point when his reality was put into context: a greater reality had arrived in Christ. Jesus did not negate John's words and actions – indeed, John "made a straight path for Him" (Mark 1:3) – rather Jesus made use of them and then exponentially outgrew them.

To be used in this manner by God is, of course, a privilege. The earthly aspects of both the preacher and his or her words must become less as Christ becomes more. The preacher's words must be prepared for transformation as the Lord makes use of them. Comedic words are especially suitable for such change and transformation. 'Shape shifting comedy' is always ready to change and even to die to make way for another reincarnation of comedy, or a different emotion, or even for the Creator of all things.

Nowhere is this truth more apparent than when we encounter the thin line that divides laughter and sadness, comedy and tragedy. How frequently comedy crumbles and dies to allow tears to flow, or horror to grip, or some other feeling take over in people's minds. The secular world has been painstaking to explore this thin line and to exploit it in theatre and entertainment for centuries. For example, commentator Philip Barnes wrote the following when he investigated playwright Alan Bennett's technique:

The majority of his plays, whether for the stage or television, tread a thin line between farcical comedy and a serious and sympathetic understanding of human life. Bennett has said about this that 'edges seem to be the most interesting thing ... it seems to me much more interesting to write about the edge between comedy and tragedy and to be able to stray from one to the other ... somehow tread the line between the two.'[78]

The extraordinarily talented comedian Richard Pryor often demonstrated not just the thin line, but the sacrificial way in which comedic dialogue moves aside to offer listeners a deeper and different experience. When Pryor died in 2005, he had achieved both fame and notoriety. His lifestyle and language were frequently negatively criticized, his talent as a comedian was not.

In reviewing 1982's *Richard Pryor Live on Sunset Strip,* a critic noted that the performance was, "often more touching than funny, it is one of the most intensely personal moments in the history of films."[79] I believe that Pryor's earlier recording of

---

[78] P. Barnes, *A Companion to Post-War British Theatre,* (Routledge, 1986), 35

[79] D. Bogle, *Toms, Coons, Mulattoes, Mammies and Bucks,* (Continuum International Publishing, 2001), 277

a live show, *Live and Smokin'*, offers an even better example of the comedian at his finest. I also believe that it reveals a precious moment of comedy bringing uncomfortable reality to the audience and dying in the process.

Live and Smokin' was filmed in 1971 at the New York City *Improvisation Nightclub*. Richard Pryor's entire routine lasts only forty-three minutes and he begins by saying that he's not sure what he's going to talk about, but has made a list of ideas to help him along. So begins a tirade of vulgar language and obscene imagery that periodically prompts much laughter and, by equal measure, prompts embarrassed silences and murmurs from the audience.

After twenty-nine minutes, Pryor enters into a routine which he himself called, "The Wino Preacher." It begins: "Hang with winos 'cos they know Jesus personally. If you died, you could go to heaven from a wino ..."[80] At this point, Pryor adopts the persona of a dishevelled, homeless alcoholic who is about to take his first drink of the day.

The imagined conversation is initially coherent and extremely funny to the audience. The routine

---

[80] *Live and Smokin'*, dir. Michael Blum, 1971 (DVD, MPI Home Video, 2001)

moves into a retelling of the life of Christ where Jesus is no longer born two thousand years ago in Bethlehem, but in the 1950s in a New York ghetto. As time goes on, however, the wino continues drinking and the speech becomes more random and intensely tragic. The dramatic arm and hand gestures are replaced by unnerving contractions and fidgets. The routine lasts fully fourteen minutes and ends the performance.

The audience initially fail to notice the death of the comedy, so subtle is the moment. After some time, the audience members, who are straining to laugh, realize that no-one else in the room is doing so. Absolute silence descends as the comedian performs and the experience is transformed. No longer are the audience a group of people enjoying an evening of escapist comedy, free for an hour or so from the 'real world' in which they live. The audience is now a group of viewers in the gallery of the Bedlam Madhouse, looking on at the antics of the insane. Next they are on the street corner that they usually hurry past, trapped by the homeless man that they either ignore or hand a dollar. Comedy has fulfilled its task and is no more.

Comedy gives way to that which is more real. In some instances, this is newer comedy; in others, tragedy or pathos; in still other instances, comedy can give way to the Good News. There are plenty of other types of utterance and presentation that are not so gracious in yielding the limelight. Many a sermon has been spoiled or muffled by self-indulgent diatribes. Some have been derailed by tangential information that actively vies for the congregation's attention or memory. Comedy yields to the Gospel having placed it deeply into the hearts and minds of the congregation – it can be used like God's disposable hypodermic needle.

III. *Engendering a conversation*. W. G. Sebald includes photographs throughout *The Rings of Saturn*. The pictures were often taken by the author himself and they are absolutely in keeping with his literary style: they are curious captured moments. Each picture is in the midst of a detailed, descriptive commentary. In all of the images contained in the book, be they photographic or drawn with words, Sebald makes no attempt to *interpret* the created image for his readers.

Far from feeling that I had engaged in a conversation, I personally likened the experience of reading *The Rings of Saturn* to solving a long, pictorial riddle. Each subdivision of each chapter quietly adds to a personal conclusion that is building like a jigsaw in the reader's mind. It is a fascinating, but lonely experience.

I find that biblical narrative engages my mind in a far more challenging and conversational manner. It is not often so quiet, nor is it so compliant. Little wonder that the writer to the Hebrews described it as, "living and active. Sharper than any double-edged sword, it penetrates even to dividing soul and spirit, joints and marrow; it judges the thoughts and attitudes of the heart" (Hebrews 4:12).

When a preacher introduces the congregation to a passage of Scripture, neither listener nor Scripture should sit in silence – a conversational interaction should begin, albeit within the mind of the listener. As Fred Craddock emphasised:

> Christian leadership sometimes demands more than introducing the text and listeners to each other; sometimes one has to get a conversation started. Interpretation seeks to do just that.[81]

Humour surrounds and infiltrates much social interaction. It sets people at ease and facilitates deeper involvement with less misunderstanding and antagonism. Eminent linguistic authorities go as far as to say that, "the transmission and

---

[81] F.B. Craddock, *Preaching*, (Abingdon Press, 1985), 150

comprehension of humour are central features of social interaction."[82]

In short, where there is conversation, there is usually humour. Why would comedy and humour not be especially supportive and welcome in the context of the congregation *conversing* with Scripture via the preaching ministry?

"I don't do comedy" said my fellow minister. The question is, should he?

It is understood that comedy usually refuses to be as rigidly defined as I have attempted in this explanation. My areas of focus and consideration are far from exhaustive, and in many circumstances do not stand alone in the manner I have portrayed them, but rather represent building blocks that go towards constructing a 'complete' moment of comedy.

A lengthier study would have included explorations of 'insult comedy' and invective; the cross cultural common ground that humour produces and the barriers to common laughter that are raised by differences in ethnicity; the gender issues that extend far beyond sexist joking and into the perception of humour itself.

---

[82] L. Anolli, R. Ciceri, G. Riva, *Say Not To Say: New Perspectives on Miscommunication*, (IOS Press, 2002), 133

I have left much unspoken, but I hope that my words have betrayed a firm belief that comedy can assist the preacher in his or her task. I also hope that my words have betrayed a love for the chimeric creature that is comedy.

With this latter point in mind, I would say to my fellow minister that he should feel free not to do comedy. At least, until he has seen beyond its common and frequently crude trappings and recognized more than a linguistic tool. Don't do comedy until you believe it to be a blessing.

Bibliography

J. E. Adams, *Preaching With Purpose*, (Zondervan Publishing, 1986)

J. Almon, *The New Foundling Hospital for Wit – being a collection of fugitive pieces, in prose and verse, not in any other collection*, (J. Debrett Publisher, 1786)

L. Anolli, R. Ciceri, G. Riva, *Say Not To Say: New Perspectives on Miscommunication*, (IOS Press, 2002)

Anon., *The Pulpit Orator; being a new selection of eloquent pulpit discourses, accompanied with observations*, (Printed for Joseph Nancrede by David Carlisle, 1804)

Aristotle, trans. W.H. Fyfe, *Poetics, Aristotle in 23 Volumes, Vol. 23*, (Heinemann, 1934)

E. Auerbach, Trans. W.R. Trask, *Mimesis: The Representation of Reality in Western Literature*, (Princeton University Press, 1968)

W. Barclay, *Daily Study Bible, The Gospel of Mark*, (The St Andrew Press, 1960)

P. Barnes, *A Companion to Post-War British Theatre*, (Routledge, 1986)

K. Barth, *Prayer and Preaching*, (London: SCM, 1964)

J. Barton and D. Muddiman (editors), *The Oxford Bible Commentary* (Oxford University Press, 2001)

D. W. Bebbington, *Evangelicalism In Modern Britain: a history from the 1730s to the 1980s*, (London: Unwin Hyman, 1989)

D. Bogle, *Toms, Coons, Mulattoes, Mammies and Bucks*, (Continuum International Publishing, 2001)

O. Borchert and L.M. Stalker, *The Original Jesus*, (James Clarke and Co., 2004)

L. O. Brastow, *Representative Modern Preachers*, (Read Books, 2007)

A. Breton, trans. M. Polizzotti, *Anthology of Black Humour*, (City Lights Books, San Francisco, 2001)

D.S. Briscoe, *Fresh Air in the Pulpit* (Inter-Varsity Press, 1994)

J. Broadus, *A treatise on the preparation and delivery of sermons*, (London: Hamilton Adams, 1874)

M. Brottman, *Funny Peculiar – Gershon Legman and the Psychopathology of Humor*, (Routledge, 2004)

F.H. Buckley, *The Morality of Laughter*, (University of Michigan Press, 2005)

F. Buechner *Telling the Truth: The Gospel as Tragedy, Comedy, and Fairy Tale*, (Harper Collins, 1977)

D. Callery, *Through the Body – a practical guide to physical theatre*, (Routledge: Theatre Arts, 2002)

A.J. Chapman, H.C Foot, P. Derks, *Humor and Laughter: Theory, Research and Applications*, (Transaction Books, 1996)

F.B. Craddock, *Preaching* (Abingdon Press, 1985)

A. S. Dale, *Comedy is a Man in Trouble*, (University of Minnesota Press, 2001)

S. V. DeLeers, *Written Text Becomes Living Word: The Vision and Practice of Sunday Preaching*, (Collegeville, MN: The Liturgical Press, 2004)

J. Drakeford *Humor in Preaching (The Craft of Preaching)*, (Zondervan, 1986)

C. E. Fant, *Bonhoeffer: Worldly Preaching* (Thomas Nelson, 1975)

B. Fife, T. Blanco, S. Kissell, B. Johnson, R. Dewey, H. Diamond, J. Wiley, G. Lee, *Creative Clowning*, (Piccadilly Books Ltd., 1992)

D. Fo, trans. S. Hood, *The Tricks of the Trade*, (Routledge, 1991)

P.T. Forsyth, *Positive preaching and modern mind* (Kessinger Publishing, 2003)

C. Fox, *The Cambridge Companion to Jonathan Swift*, (Cambridge University Press, 2003)

L. E. Francis, 'Laughter, the Best Mediation: Humor as Emotion Management in Interaction',

Symbolic Interaction, Summer 1994, Vol. 17, No. 2, Pages 147–163

K. Friedman, *Cowboy Logic – the wit and wisdom of Kinky Friedman (and some of his friends)*, (Macmillan, 2007)

D. E. Garland, *Colossians – The NIV Application Commentary*, (Zondervan Publishing House, 1998)

C. Gittings, *Death, Burial and the Individual in Early Modern England*, (Routledge Publishers, 1988)

D. M. Greenshaw and R. J. Allen, *Preaching in the Context of Worship*, (St Louis, Miss.: Chalice P., 2000)

D. Griffin, *Satire- A Critical Reintroduction*, (University Press of Kentucky, 1994)

M. J. Harris, *Exegetical Guide to the Greek New Testament: Colossians and Philemon*, (Wm. B. Eerdman's Publishing, 1991)

A. Härtner, *Learning to preach today: a guide for communicators and listeners*, (Sheffield: Cliff College Publishing, 2004)

L. Hunt, *Wit and Humor Selected from the English Poets*, (Wiley and Putnam, 1846)

G. Kittel, G. Friedrich, trans. G. W. Bromiley, *Theological Dictionary of the New Testament*, (Wm. B. Eerdman's Publishing, 1985)

H. Lockyer, *All the Parables of the Bible*, (Zondervan Publishing House, 1988)

T.G. Long, *The Witness of Preaching*, (Westminster John Knox Press, 2005)

R. A. Martin, *The Psychology of Humor: An Integrative Approach*, (Academic Press, 2006)

R. P. Martin, *Colossians: The Church's Lord and the Christian's Liberty*, (The Paternoster Press, 1972)

J. Mendrinos, *The Complete Idiot's Guide to Comedy Writing*, (Penguin, 2004)

J.P. Mitchell, *Visually Speaking* (T&T Clark Ltd., 1999)

R. Monkhouse, *Just Say A Few Words – The Complete Speaker's Handbook*, (Lennard Publishing, 1999)

H. R. Niebuhr, *Christ and Culture – 50th Anniversary Expanded Edition* (Harper San Francisco, 2001)

A. Noble, 'The Place of Preaching', in H. Rowdon (ed.), *Church Leaders Handbook* (Paternoster Press for 'Partnership', 2002)

M. Pasquarello III, *Sacred rhetoric: preaching as a theological and pastoral practice of the church*, (Grand Rapids, Michigan: Eerdmans, 2005)

R. R. Provine, *Laughter: A Scientific Investigation*, (Penguin, 2001)

P. Ricoeur, *The Conflict of Interpretations: Essays in Hermeneutics*, (Northwestern University Press, 2007)

E. Rowell and B. Steffen *Humor for Preaching and Teaching: From Leadership Journal and Christian Reader*, (Baker Books, 1998)

J. Rudlin, *Commedia Dell'arte: An Actor's Handbook* , **(Routledge, 1994)**

B. Rushing *The Art of Using Humor in Preaching: Toward A Methodology Which Equips Pastors To Use Humor Intentionally In Preaching*, (Lambert Academic Publishing, 2010)

L. Ryken, J. Wilhoit, J. C. Wilhoit, T. Longman, C. Duriez, D. Penney, D. G. Reid, *Dictionary of Biblical Imagery*, (Inter Varsity Press, 1998)

R. Schechner, *Performance Theory*, (Routledge, 2003)

D. J. Schlafer, *Your Way with God's Word: Discovering your Distinctive Preaching Voice,* (Boston Massachusetts: Cowley Publications, 1995)

F. M. Segler and R. Bradley, *Christian Worship: Its Theology and Practice*, (Broadman and Holman, 2006)

L. Siegel, *Not Remotely Controlled*, (Basic Books, 2007)

R. Smith Jr., J. E. Massey, *Doctrine That Dances: Bringing Doctrinal Preaching and Teaching to Life*, (B. and H. Publishing Group, 2008)

J. Suurmond, *Word and Spirit at Play: Towards a Charismatic Theology*, (Wm. B. Eerdman's Publishing, 1995)

G. A. Test, *Satire – Spirit and Art*, (University Press of Florida, 1991)

T. H. Troeger, *Imagining a Sermon*, (Nashville, Tenn.: Abingdon P., 1990)

R. E. Van Harn, *Pew rights: for people who listen to sermons*, (Grand Rapids, Michigan: Eerdmans, 1993)

D. O. Via, The Parables, Their Literary and Existential (Fortress Press, 1967)

J. M. Webb *Comedy and Preaching*, (Chalice Press, 1998)

J. Westerhoff, *Spiritual Life: the Foundation for Preaching and Teaching*, (Westminster: John Knox Press, 1994)

D. Worcester, *The Art of Satire*, (Russel and Russel, 1960)

Nigel G. Wright, *New Baptists, New Agenda* (Paternoster Press, 2002)

www.ingramcontent.com/pod-product-compliance
Lightning Source LLC
Chambersburg PA
CBHW061739020426
42331CB00006B/1293